PHILOSOPHY AND
THE MEANING OF LIFE

PHILOSOPHY
AND THE MEANING
OF LIFE

BY

KARL BRITTON

Professor of Philosophy
University of Newcastle upon Tyne

CAMBRIDGE

AT THE UNIVERSITY PRESS

1969

Published by the Syndics of the Cambridge University Press
Bentley House, 200 Euston Road, London N.W.1
American Branch: 32 East 57th Street, New York, N.Y.10022

Library of Congress Catalogue Card Number: 69-12926
Standard Book Numbers:
Cloth Bound: 521 07456 8
Paperback: 521 09593 x

Printed in Great Britain
at the University Printing House, Cambridge
(Brooke Crutchley, University Printer)

CONTENTS

TO MY CHILDREN

CHAPTER I

TWO RELATED QUESTIONS

❖◇❖◇❖◇❖◇❖◇❖◇❖◇❖◇❖◇❖◇❖◇❖◇❖◇❖◇❖◇❖◇❖◇❖◇❖◇❖

MEN AND WOMEN want to read philosophy because they think it will help them to understand the meaning of life: and many philosophers confess that this is what first led them to study philosophy. On the whole, however, the question of the meaning of life does not loom large in the teaching or writing of professional philosophers nowadays: and I wonder if those who turn to philosophy books or come to the university to study philosophy with this end in view would wish or expect to find that it did. What the beginner hopes (I suppose) is to have a shot at answering the question himself: but believes the study of philosophy is the best method, or only rational method, of tackling the question. In this book I shall try to decide what the question means: what could possibly count as an answer to the question: what methods can be used to find an answer. All these topics are most closely bound up with each other: and since we shall have to 'take the matter pretty deep' and ask about our conceptions not only of life and the universe but also of meaning and reason, I should regard the undertaking of the book as itself philosophical.

The question (What is the meaning of life?) is put in many different ways. What is the meaning *of it all*? What is the meaning of *everything*? What is it all in aid of? Why is there anything at all and why just what there is and not something quite different? And this connects with the wonder or fear that perhaps the part of the universe we have knowledge of is only a fragment of something which really is very different. If so, how are we to look for the reason of it all? But even if we had in the end to decide that we cannot answer the question put in this form because we have not the data, we could still go on to ask ourselves what we would count as being an answer if it could be had. On many other very large and interesting questions we have to admit that no answer can be given because we have not the data: but at least we may be quite clear what would count as an answer. To know what would count as an answer may itself be satisfying in its own way: disappointing perhaps, but neither frustrating nor humiliating. As a matter of fact it is often a considerable achievement to have reached this stage. For certainly we often ask questions without having any clear idea of what would be an answer. And we may even realise that no answer is possible before we understand why. If the question is of sufficient interest we may still want to know what impossible thing would count as an answer. It might, of course, be objected that we cannot ask a question unless we know what it means and that we cannot know what it means unless we know what would constitute an answer. This objection is either merely pedantic and unrealistic: or it serves to encourage us to try to find out what our question means.

One of the very odd things about 'the meaning of life' is that people commonly do not make a sharp distinction between a question about everything and a question about *themselves*. For the ordinary reflective person will go on: What is it all for? Why am I here? What is the point of it all? (And I suspect this often means: What is the point of it all for me?) It not only is a matter of wonder that there is this universe, but also that it contains *me*: Why am *I* here? And, of course, this connects with the question: What am I? How different might I have been or become and still be me? And since there is this universe and it includes me, what was the point of including me? Is it possible to discover in such reflections what is the point of it all for me?

There seem to be two questions, one about the universe and one about me.

Question One: Why does the universe exist? Why does something exist rather than nothing? Why the things we actually discover and not other possible things?

Question Two: Why do I exist? Do I exist for some purpose, and, if so, how am I to discover it?

These two questions are referred to again and again throughout the book. They are closely connected and many of the central problems discussed have to do with their connexion.

Ought we to try to make a sharp distinction between a question about the world and a question about me? On the face of it they seem to belong to quite different orders. If I think of the universe—of what there is altogether—then one might well suppose that the last thing that could be of importance for understanding the

3

universe would be—me. (And at the same time one might see it as a characteristic aberration to think of oneself as an important consideration in every problem whatever.) But this is to consider the universe as a going concern: as having an age and a size and a structure in which I certainly am too insignificant to be mentioned. However, some people raise a prior question: Why should there *be* anything at all? And they profess to find that they can raise the same question about each single thing that actually exists—including themselves. Of course in a sense I know already why I exist: I was conceived and was born and have survived until now. But children are also sometimes told that God makes each one of us. This is a way of saying that—our parents notwithstanding—there is or ought to be some reason for each of us existing not as offspring but as ourselves. So that one of the reasons why 'the meaning of life' is both about the universe and about ourselves, is that we do not have to regard the existence of other things in the universe as a full, perfect and sufficient reason for the existence of any single thing—myself for example.

Another reason is that all my knowledge about the world comes to me through my own experience of it: including in this experience the books I have read and the teaching and conversations that I have had. I have come to know something of the world because I can see and hear and touch and imagine and reason. In one sense, of course, I can occupy only a very minor position in this all-comprehending world. But in another sense I comprehend the world: it is the world as I know it that I want

4

explained. I am not asking for the further elaboration of a possible world: but for some account of the existing world. And the existing world is the one which I have had some experience of. It includes me. Before I was born the world had long presented problems to other minds but not to me. The twenty-second century will not be our problem at the time. But meanwhile the whole (past, present and future) is a problem for me because I know about it. Therefore, to ask my question about the universe is to ask a question about my own existence. Had I never been born I should have had no problem. When Job wished that he had been carried from the womb to the grave no doubt it was partly because he would have avoided God's wrath: but also I think because he would have avoided the terrible question of why he had been brought into existence at all.

The two questions are really connected: to find out about the world one must distinguish the world from oneself: and conversely. We know that infants have to learn to make this distinction: and it is often said that we tend to confuse the two; commonly in our day-dreaming and sometimes in our more serious thinking. That I imagine things is a truth about me: what I imagine is very often not true of the world. 'It is a common observation that the mind has a great propensity to spread itself on external objects.' This crude statement of David Hume's is uncontrovertible.[1]

This connexion leads me to the view that 'The

[1] Hume: *Treatise of Human Nature*, Book I, Part iii, § 14.

Meaning of Life' is a practical problem. Certainly the second question *looks* practical: Why am I here? What is the point of it all? It looks as though an answer to this question is needed in order to decide how to live. I do not deny that one could treat the first version (or the first question) in a purely theoretical spirit. Children may be led by pure curiosity to ask how the sea came to be there: and physicists how metals came to be there: so others may be curious to know how everything came to be here. I shall discuss this kind of interest in Chapter 5: which is something of a diversion from my main topic. Because what really concerns me is the two questions asked in the same breath—as they so often are by people who do not seem to notice that they are making a switch from the universe to themselves. I believe this association is important and indicates that the motive of the question is not curiosity but rather bewilderment about what it is all for: and so, how am I to live—for what reasons, to what end, in what manner?

Whose questions are these? I think all reflective people ask these questions at some time or another: I want to mention some of the people in particular.

Those who are growing up: who begin to see both the extent of their own capacities and weaknesses and the formidable size, history, age, and power of the external world. They are still in process of sorting out the one from the other. They are busy unlearning much that they have been taught about both. They are engaged in disengaging themselves from their parents and families and teachers.

6

In Protestant countries this stage of life tends to take on a strongly intellectual character: as though there must be an intellectual clean slate before adult life can begin.[1] They may well ask: What am I up against in this world? What may I live by? What am I to live for? It would be quite impossible here to separate theoretical questions from practical bewilderment, if only because at such a stage one may want simply to know about things because they are interesting—and even about oneself as a thing. But even those whose strongest bent is for theoretical enquiries do not necessarily give up their questions about how to live. They may turn to physics or biology or history and become thoroughly absorbed in them. But it remains possible that they believe that the questions they ask about the world have a bearing on practical questions about the meaning of life.

Growing up at some stage means taking a job. This certainly is a practical matter. Many hope that they will find the meaning of life in their work, especially if they have chosen their own job. But I think there is a very important stage to be passed through. The job disappoints: in a sense it is bound to do so, simply because it was not designed to satisfy the worker but for some other end. So that in one's first or second or third job one has to face the fact that a certain amount of adaptation or adjustment is necessary. And this is commonly felt as an affront to one's individuality or dignity as a person. (Of course in many cases it is unnecessarily and avoidably so.) It seems to me that this is often a moment of truth: whatever else

[1] Cf. William James: *Varieties of Religious Experience*, Chapter IV.

one may say about the world, quite evidently it was not simply made for me. There is me and there is the world. Naturally, the question has more poignancy for those who fail in their work. It is easy to dismiss such people as having a chip on their shoulders: and this can be a cosmic chip.[1] It can appear very early in life. Those who have 'missed the boat' in this life may at least feel that they have learned a thing or two that success might have hidden from them. (Might have, for it is possible, of course, to contemplate all this imaginatively without experiencing it.) What is it men suppose they have learned? Not merely that the world was not designed for me: but that it was not designed for justice.

Would anybody suppose that it was or could be designed for justice were it not for the traditional doctrine that God is just? Would anybody nowadays think up such a view afresh? It is clearly connected with the fact that every society has a system of justice: making some distinction between those of ill-desert and those of good desert. And we come to see that even on a society's own conceptions the bad are often rewarded and the good discarded and humiliated. Moreover, society's conceptions are very limited: it takes little reason or imagination to see that there are merits and demerits ignored by the system. We are led to generalise, to widen and deepen the notion of justice. Nothing in society at large corresponds to this notion. And this, if experienced personally, may be a great sense of disillusionment. But why then should any-

[1] 'A cosmic chip': a phrase I owe to a postcard from Professor Gilbert Ryle.

8

one be surprised to find *nature* unjust? We commonly make a sharp distinction between natural and moral evils. Accidents, loss of ability, disease, deformity, provoke sadness but not that anger and resentment typical of human actions that are malicious or unjust. Mill's remark: 'Nearly all the things which men are hanged or imprisoned for doing to one another, are nature's everyday performances', sounds very unconvincing.[1] If nature includes only the natural contingencies then we can say that nature is in a sense unfair: that is, it pays no regard whatever to good desert and ill-desert. There is a natural order but this does not exclude two processes going on side by side, each according to the law of its nature, but without any order or connexion between the two. So men lead good or bad lives and they enjoy good or bad fates. Nothing regularly correlates the two. If the good man is overcome by disaster this is a coincidence: if the bad man lives out his days in happiness and honour this is also a coincidence. It is possible, however, to believe that there ought to be a connexion.

How is it possible to believe this? We do not always make a correct distinction between what men do to us and what simply happens to us. We blame other people (as we also often blame ourselves) for what is really accidental. But this still presupposes that we are making a distinction. Is it possible both to see that something is accidental and to resent it as unjust? Is it possible to feel that I personally am a *victim* of circumstances?—to believe that some force has singled me out for evil or for good?—

[1] J. S. Mill: *Three Essays on Religion* (on Nature), p. 28.

that fate is really against me or that good luck is on my side? Such thinking may be primitive but it certainly is very common: that is to say we can and often do (some perhaps not quite seriously, others very seriously) feel that nature is treating us unjustly. This has led many people to say: Unless the balance is restored and justice done outside this life, then there is no meaning in this life. I suppose that most of those who actually believe that justice *will* be done in another life, do so on religious grounds: and some might say that whether it involves a belief in a just God or not, it is itself a religious belief. I am not trying to decide any such point at present. But I want to insist that for very many people a belief in a just order of nature is a kind of practical necessity. Of course, a man cannot decide to believe what he knows to be impossible: but I suppose we often decide to believe what we know to be very doubtful. This I think is why many people, reflecting on the injustice of this life, decide that its meaning must be found in another world than ours.

Is such a belief commoner amongst the old or the young? No doubt the old have a different ground for thinking of an after-life. As death comes near, an end may seem more and more unwelcome. But even if (as I think is often the case) it becomes more and more acceptable, there is no doubt that its approach brings many reasons for further reflection on the meaning of life. For one thing we cannot understand life unless we really face the fact of death. Where did I come from? Where am I going to? And this is also the time for looking back and seeing what (if anything) one's own life now adds up to: what point or pattern now appears in it. With this is connected our sense of responsibility for what we have (through all hazards) actually done with our lives.

> Greater glory in the sun,
> An evening chill upon the air,
> Bid imagination run
> Much on the Great Questioner;
> What He can question, what if questioned I
> Can with a fitting confidence reply.

Yeats's *Meditation upon Death* at Algeciras, is not itself a dogmatic poem: and its temper of dignity and assurance is not Christian. It does not in itself imply anything about an after-life. But it poses a question about life in a way that is typical of one of its important stages.

I have said that these questions are asked by all thought-ful people: and particularly by the young and by those who are nearing the end of life; by those faced with difficult choices and those who feel their lives have been a failure or that life has treated them unjustly. I think it is important to add a special class: the question of who I am, has particular point for a person who is mentally unstable. An answer to the question: What is the meaning of life, seems to presuppose some settled notion of what I am, what a person is. Because the meaning must be for me or for somebody. If a person suffers from some mental disorder he may, in fact, find it hard to think of himself as a continuing person at all. There is nothing new about this phenomenon: and since mental disorders and high intelligence often go together, we can assume that this is a problem that has always been facing some people. If the question What is the meaning of life? has somewhat changed, I think it is on account of our new recognition of mental instability. It has not changed fundamentally: but now our answer must take account of this most urgent of personal perplexities if only because for the first time we are allowed to talk about it and have something of a vocabulary to use.

Should professional philosophers bother with the question of the meaning of life? It is not long since the hard-faced business-man of philosophy met such questions with questions of his own. Is the answer verifiable? Can the terms be made clear? Why bother with such a logically odd use of *meaning*? (Words and sentences have meaning, not life or the universe.) I think we should in the main ignore these objections; because the Adversary put too easy questions. Vague, nebulous, provocative though it may be, I do not believe that 'the meaning of life' is a senseless term; and I believe it can be connected with many more tractable, clearer questions. But if they can be answered at all, it may be in part by decisions: because they are at bottom of a practical not a speculative nature. To say that there is a meaning in life is to say that there is something that may serve as a guide in our lives.

First of all, we are saying that we find some things worth while on their own account and that we can make these things our aim. Whether we succeed or not, life will not be pointless or meaningless: we *could* succeed. This looks rather like saying that life has a meaning if we give it one. But this is not really the case, because we cannot arbitrarily assert that this or that is worth while on its own account. We must, and usually do, give reasons: and if this giving reasons ends up by appeal to a principle for which no reason can be given, then we must at least claim that this basic principle is generally or at the very least widely accepted. Or (to pursue the matter to the bitter end) we must claim that it ought to be generally accepted. We do not make things valuable by our choice: we identify things as valuable and we can be mistaken in doing this and discover our mistakes. So that certain things (of whose existence or possible existence we learn by experience) are worth while in themselves: this is an evaluation but it is not an arbitrary choice. For there might have been nothing that we could say had value for its own sake: or (if that seems absurd) nothing that could help us to decide how to live our own lives. In that case we might *wish* that life had a meaning but in fact it would have none. To say that life has a meaning if we wish it had a meaning is nonsensical: it illustrates a form of inference which can at once be seen to be invalid (wishes are not horses and beggars do not ride). We are considering not a wish but a discovery.

However, people do in fact identify different things as having value in themselves in the long run. (I say 'in the long run' because we are speaking of things we may guide our lives by, and whether this is a long run or a short run it is at all events the *whole* run.) Consider G. E. Moore's view that the things that are *by far* the greatest goods we know or can conceive, are personal affection and the contemplation of beautiful objects.[1] Moore did not offer this as an argument about the meaning of life (which he did not discuss): but as a most important truth which we may all recognise but for which argument is neither necessary nor possible. Are we to say that anyone who acknowledges the truth of this view believes that the meaning of life lies in friendship and in the beauty of nature and art? But that if one disagreed with Moore's view, and held that the greatest goods we know or can imagine are moral integrity and compassion, then one would hold a different and disagreeing view as to the meaning of life? And we ought here to add: What of Sardanapallus? He held that the only things that mattered in life were sensual pleasures and especially eating.[2] Are we to say that these three views as to what is most worth pursuing in life entail these quite different views of what the meaning of life is?

We are certainly tempted to say so. And if we do, we must admit that the claim that we know what the meaning of life is, rests simply on our own moral convictions: other people have other convictions and although we feel they are mistaken, we have to admit that the question: What is the meaning of life? cannot be given an agreed answer.

Such a view is not vacuous; there might have been nothing (or nothing man could even attempt) which *anyone* could regard as worth while in the long run. In

[1] G. E. Moore: *Principia Ethica*, Chapter VI, p. 188, and opening remarks on the Summum Bonum, p. 183 etc.

[2] Sardanapallus: See Aristotle, *Nicomachean Ethics*, Book I, Chapter 5.

fact, there are different things which different people regard as of value in the long run. But so long as my moral convictions hold, at all events I can claim that I have settled the question and that other views are mistaken.

To adopt this interpretation implies that G. E. Moore and J. S. Mill, who offered us no 'metaphysic of ethics', and who perhaps hardly attached any sense to the question (What is the meaning of Life?), nevertheless provided answers to the question—disagreeing answers. For they may be understood to say that the meaning of life is shown in friendship and beauty—or in increasing the sum of happiness in the world. Both have would rejected Sardanapallus (as Aristotle did) as a joke in bad taste. Would Moore deny that Mill had found the correct answer to the question of what the meaning is? If he accepted the question he would have to do so. That they did not even discuss the question in these terms makes us wonder if they understood it in some other sense: if they thought the question involved other considerations altogether. What would these be? Something about a purpose *for man*. And it is worth mentioning that neither has much to say about the whole of life—which of course includes death.

For life to have a meaning some conditions may be necessary without being sufficient. To get a university degree it is necessary to study and to sit the examinations. But these two conditions are still not sufficient: there are people who study and sit the examinations but do not qualify for degrees. One has also to *pass* the examinations. Are these three taken together sufficient conditions for getting a degree? It seems that they are. I am suggesting that for life to have a meaning it is necessary that there should be some things worth doing for their own sakes. But is this sufficient? Some might say that it is: from which we infer that this is all that *they* understand by life's having a meaning. Others will say that while this is a necessary condition it is not a sufficient condition. This indicates that they give a wider, ampler meaning to the expression 'the meaning of life'. What could this further condition be?

Clearly one might think of the meaning of life as something which some power not ourselves *has put before us to pursue*. Of course one could imagine a featureless god who set before men some goal and somehow drove them to pursue it. (This is the account given by some forms of Christian theology.) But in this case, while I might admit that in a sense the goal explains how I came to be here, for what end, yet I could recognise all this and still say: It leaves life without meaning. The goal would seem arbitrary, senseless: and its pursuit burdensome, soul-destroying. It would in some ways be like the rat-race: we find ourselves made to struggle (we do not understand why) for some achievement we do not value; and to extract oneself from the race may be difficult or impossible. This surely is a meaningless existence. So that even if I acknowledged the fact that men are here to struggle and suffer for some alien purpose, I could reject the purpose—a free man would reject it. This shows that a system of means and ends in nature is not by itself sufficient to endow life with meaning: but is it a necessary condition?

It seems that the question about the meaning of life may have a double reference. Is there in life a goal set before me by nature, by god, by some power not myself: and is it a goal I can accept as worth while on its own account —a goal which I am led to follow by recognising that *both* these conditions hold?

I think many people shrink from even discussing the second condition:[1] and hold either that life has a meaning if I find long-term goals worth pursuing for their own sake—that this is *all that is needed* for the conclusion that life has a meaning: or they pass by the question altogether. People shrink from asking it partly because it seems incapable of an answer based on experience: it has a transcendental (outside-this-world) air. Many also hold that a rational being ought to determine his fundamental aims without reference to what anyone else may have chosen for him. Even if we knew God or nature had set us a goal, that would not in itself be a reason for adopting the goal.[2]

Why do people persist in pressing the second half of the question? Why does it not seem enough to say: Life is in fact able to show things worth aiming at, worth devoting a lifetime to?

[1] See below, Chapter 2, pp. 21–9 and Chapter 9, pp. 192–4.
[2] Kant: *Fundamental Principles of the Metaphysic of Ethics*, trans. Abbott, p. 74. (All references are to this translation.)

First, because there is not agreement about what these things are. In discussing 'the ends of life' we evince the hope that we might come to agreement. God is brought in not to uncover the correct view, but to be the absolute standard of reference by which it is defined. Even one who concludes that he does not know the meaning can suppose there *is* a meaning. This too is different from the view that there is no standard whatever for determining the matter.

Secondly, because people really do sometimes feel *driven* to a view as to what is worth while. I mean that they cannot explain why they hold it, why they cannot accept alternatives. It feels as if the answer to the question comes from outside, overcoming everyday objections, ignoring everyday questions. And one might well say: I have no idea how I should decide such a question if it were ever put to me: but fortunately *it is decided for me*. And I do not mean that I accept from fear or emulation; but in all good faith. It is as though one acknowledges that other views can be formulated but they simply count for nothing. Something like this leads people to say: This is the goal I was born for.

Thirdly, to determine on a goal which shapes our lives is to set forth on a journey and this needs confidence. At its crudest one might say: I should not accept this goal unless I believed I had a chance of achieving it. And this already implies that nature, the world, permits my success. This seems to imply some limitation on what we may expect to face. It is a characteristically religious belief that, bad as things may be, they will never be too dreadful for us to bear; there will always be some way out and finding it is a matter of purity and simplicity of heart, not cleverness. Such a faith is not empty: it is obvious that many people who once held it have been led to abandon it. Certainly we do not *know* that these things will never happen to us.

I think anyone who can make the double assertion may be said to have found a meaning in life: that is, a goal worth while for its own sake and not impossible to man: a goal set for him by God or nature, not simply picked out by his own efforts. One of the really big questions is whether the second assertion can ever reasonably be made. And in this connexion we have to ask whether the first assertion without the second is to count as an assertion about 'the meaning of life'. Here I want to point out that even the first assertion involves some view of the facts: there are goals worth pursuing for their own sake—and these, or some of these, are not impossible to man. In asking about the meaning of life we are implicitly asking what we can do, and what we are up against, and what we may live by. And of course a negative conclusion—that we alone make our choice—is itself a view of the facts. But while questions of fact are involved, they cannot be considered from a purely theoretical point of view. We want to have an answer we can act upon—before it is too late to act. We must make up our minds one way or the other.[1]

This gives our conclusions an absolute character. We

[1] See Chapter 9, pp. 194-5.

have a life at stake: a decision (although it can be abandoned) is made for life. I see other people making other decisions: and I can consider the reasons they offer, as they can consider my reasons. I am strongly inclined to believe that their decisions rest upon some kind of mistake—not that their decisions refer to a different situation. That would be a very serious conclusion to have to reach: it is a strong pull to believe that if only we could understand fully we are (at bottom) in the same situation. It is the meaning of life that is in question: not my style of living.[1]

It is then a matter of coming to terms with *everything*. This might seem presumptuous: is it not enough to try to come to terms with oneself? I think not. This would be to make a distinction between oneself and the world that is empty because only one side of the boundary is being taken seriously. To take oneself seriously (and in a certain sense we must all do this if we reflect) is to consider both sides of the barrier. Hence the question is about myself and the world: nothing is left out.

[1] Wittgenstein seems to challenge this belief: 'The world of the happy man is a different one from that of the unhappy man' (*Tractatus Logico-Philosophicus*, 6. 43). Cf. Chapter 6, pp. 139–40 and Wordsworth's lines.

CHAPTER 2

SOME AUTHORITATIVE ANSWERS

◇◇

I PROPOSE to discuss three traditional answers to the two questions: the first is the view that God has a beneficent plan for the world as a whole which can be carried out only if each person finds and completes that part of the plan which God has assigned to him. I shall call this the Protestant view. The second answer is based on the notion of God's glory and man's depravity. The world as we know it exists as an expression of God's glory: men and women are included because, being sinful, they need redemption and redemption is the supreme expression of God's glory. The third view is a much less definite one: we exist in the world in order to prepare ourselves for another life—a life after death. The world we know seems unintelligible and unjust: it is so unless it is considered as a part of a larger whole: and once we grasp this fact we can see a point in our present lives—we can know why we are here and what we should make our aim.

All three views presuppose an after-life: the first two presuppose the existence of God. The third view very commonly also presupposes the existence of God but need not do so. With this reservation the answers here discussed rest upon these two beliefs. They were formulated at a time when these beliefs were very generally accepted and have been 'handed down' as corollaries of these traditional beliefs. I call the answers *authoritative* because they rest upon traditional beliefs and I do not mean to imply that they could flourish only in an authoritarian society. (This may be true of the second but not of the other two.)

A traditional belief is one generally taught to children. These two beliefs (in God and immortality) were traditional in western society until a few generations ago. Consider the simple fact that had we been born a few generations earlier we should almost certainly have accepted these beliefs without any open discussion. And I mean that we should have believed that there is a God and that there is an after-life, not that we should have pretended to believe. This is a purely historical statement and of course I am not offering an unqualified universal proposition. There have been throughout the history of Christianity many agnostics and many unbelievers— including celebrated churchmen and perhaps one Pope. But it was generally held that these beliefs were so natural and obvious that if they were to be disputed the burden of argument rested squarely on the doubters and not on the believers. Probably even many of the doubters accepted that position. Nor is the existence of doubters a matter which need trouble the believers. Some people today deny that anyone is really responsible for his voluntary actions: hence that punishment is an empty and misleading notion. The existence of such doubters does not trouble most people. Some people hold that we can have precognition of future events: but this view (in itself very disturbing indeed to so much that we all believe) is by most people dismissed as some sort of illusion or deception. And it is certainly held that the burden of argument rests upon the nonconformists and not upon us.

Doubts about God and immortality were in past generations associated in the public mind with moral cynicism and scepticism. It seemed that the doubters were also saying: How we live does not really matter. They were apt to be called 'scoffers' as well as infidels. They were supposed to have unacknowledged and disreputable reasons for denying God and Judgement, Heaven and Hell. (And no doubt we could find many of whom this was true.) In the general mind these beliefs were the great foundation of morality and even of public order and decency. It seemed that those who denied (or doubted strongly enough) God and God's government here and hereafter would be left without any reason for trying to lead a moral life except the fear of punishment by society and the state. Hence to be taught morality beyond the purely imperative level of *do this* and *stop that*, implied being taught about God and his commandments; and about an after-life of reward or punishment. Even Bishop Butler, who recognised many other reasons for being moral, said that a belief in divine sanctions was 'our only security of persevering in our duty, in cases of great temptations'.[1] We all have to be taught morality: the state and society are there to see that (within limits) we adhere to it. The first nonconformists of our era were therefore bound to be classed with reprobates and cynics

[1] Bishop Butler: *Sermons*, XII.

even if, in fact, they were neither. This close connexion also explains why the two beliefs are or were *traditional*. The practical necessity (which is normal) of behaving properly and living morally became attached to these beliefs as to no others. We might compare the once generally accepted belief that the sun goes round the earth. In the long run this has been abandoned in favour of the view of Copernicus and Galileo, without any noticeable change in morality. It is true that the Inquisition at first condemned the new views because the older had become so tied up with theological beliefs. But the connexion of the astronomy with the theology was not really a logical connexion, and this in due course was recognised. Did the new view about the motion of the sun really have any bearing on doing justice or loving mercy or receiving the sacrament? No. But the new view about God and divine judgement did have bearing: there were logical connexions, although not as direct as was once supposed.

I have said that the beliefs were traditional: and in this sense the answers (which certainly logically presuppose these beliefs) are traditional too. But traditional beliefs are not simply handed on from generation to generation: they are also explained and defended on logical grounds. What learned men (and these even in England even a hundred years ago were mostly clerics) wished was that the beliefs should be widely understood and reasonably accepted. They therefore offered arguments for them, especially arguments against unbelievers. And I think it is quite obvious that these beliefs, as considered by highly intelligent and learned and critical minds, seemed far more plausible two hundred years ago than they do now. I mean there were then grounds for accepting them that appealed to thoroughly reasonable people: grounds which in many cases have now gone.

Of course, it would be odd to call a belief 'authoritative' or 'traditional' if one held it to be manifestly true and incontrovertible. In my opinion there is not and never was a solid ground in logic for either of these two beliefs: I mean that viewed in a purely rational way the considerations which were offered in their support are not very strong. But the fact is that they seemed to be very strong to earlier generations and to many of the most able and critical minds. How could it be that what seemed to be very good grounds for these beliefs no longer seem so to many people? How can such a change come about?

In two ways: (i) A certain type of argument once generally accepted is seen to be fallacious. For example, it is seen that we can never argue from the *notion* of a thing directly to its existence. This was the generally accepted view with regard to 'finite essences'; but in the one case of God it was held that the argument is valid. Hume and Kant tried to show that it is never valid and many people now accept this view.[1] This means that the belief in God's existence has lost this defence or ground: it does not mean that the belief has been disproved, since

---

[1] Hume: *Dialogues concerning Natural Religion*. Hume: *Enquiry concerning Human Understanding*, § 11. Kant: *Critique of Pure Reason*, The Dialectic, Book II, Chapter III.

there are, of course, other grounds on which it is held. One could take as another example the argument from design in the universe: Hume holds that this type of argument cannot be applied to the origins of the universe itself. In both cases the Hume–Kant view is not now accepted by everybody but is very widely accepted. (ii) A belief may rest upon other beliefs which, *if true*, would render it probable, perhaps overwhelmingly probable. For example, a belief is defended as an inference from certain evidence. But it can happen that the evidence itself ceases to be credible. If so, the first belief loses some of the grounds upon which it was held or by which it was defended. The difference from the first case is simply that there what changed was a view of the validity of the argument: here no doubt is thrown on the validity—if the premises were true they would support the belief. The doubt is about the truth of the premises.

The belief in an after-life was defended in the past by narratives of the appearances of the ghosts of dead people. If these stories were true it seemed reasonable to suppose that they lent some support to a belief in an after-life of some sort. Such stories were once generally accepted: today many people reject them all. A parallel point can be made about belief in God and stories of miracles. In each case the belief, even for many people who still hold it, has lost important logical grounds. Of course, while some evidence may be dismissed, new evidence may come to light. One can only say that, other things being equal, the beliefs are logically weakened.

In both cases (i) and (ii) those who have changed their

minds hold that the beliefs never were logically supported by these particular reasons, although they seemed to be so. And of course one might be puzzled by this feature in the case of changes of the second type. People believed in the ghosts and the miracles of their own day—not in all such stories but in some. Who are we to decide that they were all mistaken in their beliefs? What experiences of our day can possibly have any bearing upon these beliefs of theirs? How is it that a whole mass of evidence that seemed perfectly good evidence to other ages can now be rejected?

One way of explaining this would be to say that the second case is not really different in kind from the first. In the first case, reflexion of a logical kind showed that a certain type of argument was invalid. We may come to this conclusion now (following Hume and Kant): but if we come to hold that this type of argument is invalid now, then of course we must say that it always *was* invalid. At one blow, all previous arguments of this type fall to the ground. And it is arguable that what is now held by many people about the evidence of ghosts and miracles, is that these narratives are themselves conclusions which were drawn in the past from certain premises. And what many now really hold is that matters of observation cannot support a conclusion about 'the supernatural'. The reflexion which leads to this view cannot be called purely logical: it involves our view of natural laws, which again depends upon our view of the natural sciences. The reflection is *a priori*: that is, it is not a matter of considering afresh all the observations upon which miracles and ghost stories were founded—an impossible and end-less task. It is a matter of considering afresh a *type* of argument: although I doubt if the type could be de-scribed (as the argument from essence to existence can) in purely logical terms.

This explanation allows that what has altered is not our view as to the logical argument from miracles to God, or from ghosts to an after-life: this need not be affected. But it shows that neither miracles nor ghosts are reached without argument: and the type of argument in which these are reached is no longer acceptable. And that does entail that all past narratives of this kind, as well as present and future ones, are to be dismissed.

But I feel sure there is another very important factor in the case. We are naturally more inclined to accept a narrative if it supports a view we strongly hold, than if it counters it. This can be quite logical and reasonable; it has an initial plausibility which the contrary story has not. I say *can be* logical because it all depends upon why we are so strongly attached to the view which the narrative supports. And here I would say that in past ages it has not been so easy to look at theological propositions in a purely theoretical way. So that a very acute and critical thinker who considered them might be acute and critical in a way that is different from what we now commonly mean by these words. He would be more alive to the practical consequences of his belief than many people are now required to be. The reason for this I have already tried to give: it was because a belief in God and His Judgement

28

was regarded as essential to morality and to society. And this is only the very fringe of a big topic; while a certain narrow border of logical doctrine is recognisable throughout the writings of theologians and philosophers of the Greek–Jewish–Christian tradition (and grows and changes in ways the Greeks would have understood), these logical doctrines are not the only criteria by which arguments have been judged. Aesthetic considerations—with their own systematic demands—have been used. And I am not referring to the great army of charlatans but to outstanding thinkers of the past; and of course to many acute and critical thinkers of the modern age—to Coleridge, for example.

When I call these answers authoritative, then, I mean that they rest on beliefs which have been taught in our society, have been regarded as practically necessary: this general acceptance did not exclude analysis, explanation and criticism, but certainly did not depend upon it. And I have tried to show how it has happened that these beliefs *appeared* to be very strongly supported in logic: and that to many people they no longer seem to have just this logical support although they may still seem to be logically supported on other grounds.

I begin with what I call the Protestant answer, which seems to me to be authoritative in the sense explained, and to be an answer. It tells us why everything is here: and in particular why I am here and what I am to do with my life. I consider it first because I think it is now too little discussed and too easily dismissed: and because it still has

2-2

a great influence in the contemporary world, in Protestant and in Catholic countries: among unbelievers (perhaps in a modified form) as well as believers.

God made the world: that is why it is here. It springs from God's will. We can see much in the world that is rational and even good: but the answer to our question cannot be completed in terms of what seems to us reasonable or good. Finally, we have to say: *it must be good*, because God willed it. All sorts of ingenious concessions and explanations may be offered: but I suppose in the last resort the world's existence is 'explained' by reference to the inscrutable will of God. This is taken to be an absolute.

God made our spirits and to each he has assigned a special task or way of life: God has a plan for the world and it requires the willing co-operation of all created spirits. We cannot doubt that there is a *point* to our being here: the world would *not* be better without us: there is something we must do now in the time of this mortal life. And God gives us the means to do this task. After death 'the fire shall try every man's work of what sort it is'.

God is a working God with a moral purpose: and this purpose needs the help of men and women. This is certainly authoritarian but it is not degrading: it offers every man a good reason for his existence and an aim in life. Each is called by God to some task: he must find out and pursue his calling. No serious-minded person can be content to disregard this. Whatever else life may offer, nothing can really profit a man who neglects to discover or to follow his calling. I think this notion still influences many people even though they would not express it in theological language. It is not to be laughed off as 'Victorian earnestness': it is not peculiar to the Victorians nor incompatible with a sense of humour. My main point is that this notion of God needing us to do certain things, to lead a certain kind of life, provides an answer to the second question: a final answer.

There are three questions I wish to raise about this answer:

(i) God is presented as a task-master who demands certain things of us in return for a certain gift or talent—perhaps a very modest one. *Are we to be paid by results*? Does God make allowances for our weaknesses and failures: does the task-master recognise that we are very often childish, inept, absent-minded? Does God accept us for what we really are?

(ii) How are we to discover our 'calling'? This is clearly a very important question. How does it stand with the man who makes a mistaken choice or never manages to make a choice at all? This difficulty goes back to the parable of the talents.

(iii) Is it a coherent answer? Can we really accept the view that God needs our help to complete his plan?

(i) The parable of the talents was perhaps too much emphasised by Protestant preachers.[1] Obviously it shows a certain rough justice: the great man expects from each of his servants some reasonable return on what was lent: the results are fairly proportioned to the opportunity.

[1] St Matthew, Chapter 25.

And this lesson was certainly not neglected. The parable is reasonable and business-like. But it needs to be set against the story of the other great man who took on hands to work in his vineyard at different times of the day: and yet paid each of them a penny.[1] This at least shows that God's ways are not simply those of the business man: that our relation to God is not simply that of employee to employer. The good man of the house declines to be bound by union rules. Payment seems to take into account willingness to serve as well as service actually performed. This allows the argument that the man who did not discover his calling until the eleventh hour may yet be rewarded because he waited for it: 'They also serve who only stand and wait.' Since (as in ii) it may not be easy to discover one's calling, this is a most important consideration: were it omitted the doctrine would be pretty bleak.

(ii) How are we to discover our calling? Two very celebrated sonnets of Milton's are based upon the parable of the talents: but the second makes reference also to the parable of the vineyard.

At the age of twenty-three, Milton laments that his late spring 'no bud or blossom showeth'. But he goes on to say that as he grows up (whether faster or slower than others) he is still somehow being led onward towards that task which God has assigned to him in this life.

> Yet be it less or more, or soon or slow,
> It shall be still in strictest measure ev'n
> To that same lot, however mean or high,

[1] St Matthew, Chapter 20.

32

> Toward which Time leads me, and the will of Heav'n:
> All is, if I have grace to use it so,
> As ever in my great task Master's eye.

This is stated without argument and without question: it is what it is decent and proper for a young person to feel at this stage of life. He may not yet have found his calling but he will do so: and will then work as under God's eye.

The later sonnet on his blindness makes the same sort of point even more explicitly in the octave. It seems that God did indeed give him one talent: but then took away his sight. To hide his talent is death.

> Doth God exact day-labour, light denied,
> I fondly ask.

There is a serious bewilderment. Milton had discovered that one gift and surely it must be his calling to employ it to the full. So far we see a continuation of the theme of the earlier sonnet: the difficulty of discovering one's calling. At twenty-three this is not yet critical; but when doubts are cast on many years of activity, it is critical. Milton in the sestet finds an answer derived from the other parable: 'They also serve who only stand and wait.' This is what in the poem he represents himself as now being obliged to do. But it counts as service—just as the unemployed labourers found their waiting counted as service.

It looks, then, as though the answer can be presented in humane terms: if we cannot *find* our calling we can at least look for it or simply wait for it. This admits that the idea of a working God who has a task for each of us does

33

not guarantee that the task will be identified—or performed. This, God understands and takes into account. However, the difficulty cannot be dismissed as unimportant to the answer as stated. Why am I here? To perform some task assigned to me by God. This is my calling. It is not for nothing that the word 'calling' was used to mean employment or profession. But now it appears that I may never discover this task, or may discover too late to carry it out. I think many people who are perplexed by the second question would find comfort in the reflexion that there *is* a task for which one must look or wait. One's life is not unnecessary to God's scheme: but God does not justify us simply by our actual achievements. (The labourers who had borne the heat of the day wished to be judged by their achievements but were not.) But if God needs the work, what happens if I fail to identify it? We are told this is not in the sight of God to count as failure: but it leaves us with an odd answer to the question: Why am I here? For some purpose of God's—but what?

(iii) How did Milton reach his conclusion in the second sonnet? He argues:

> God doth not need
> Either man's work or his own gifts; who best
> Bear his mild yoke, they serve him best; his State
> Is Kingly. Thousands at his bidding speed
> And post o'er land and ocean without rest:
> They also serve who only stand and wait.

Now this seems to me to show a certain strain or even incoherence. *God doth not need.* What then is the real

34

reason for our undertaking his work? Milton, who still feels responsible about God's purposes, can take honest comfort in the thought that they are not going to suffer from his own enforced and unwilling idleness. But if God does not really need our work, why does he ask it and why should we do it?

Milton's comfort is found in a Quietist doctrine. To *be* rather than to *do* is the important thing. To bear the yoke, to obey God, is what really matters. And no doubt he would have assumed that we need no *reason* for obeying God.

This version of the answer may be a step foward in religion and in morality. Mary McCarthy, when first she attended her grandfather's church, heard the preacher announce as his text:

What doth the Lord require of thee but to do justly, and to love mercy, and to walk humbly with thy God?

There, she says, spoke the authentic voice of Protestantism.[1] Our 'calling' on this version is not a particular job, a particular contribution needed for the completion of a great work: it is simply to lead a moral life, a righteous life, for its own sake (or 'as a service to God') in whatever job and in whatever tight corners we may find ourselves. This noble, moral and humane doctrine (one which David Hume seems not to have come across) is, however, very general. It seems to imply that I am to live a righteous life *whatever my calling may be*. The golden words of the prophet Micah affirm that there is a purpose for our lives,

[1] Micah, Chapter 6, v. 8. Mary McCarthy, *Memories of a Catholic Girlhood*.

not in terms of a certain piece of work, but in terms of a certain way of living.

It might be objected that the first version is too literal-minded: that our notion of man and his place in the universe can hardly be expected to imply how this or that man should spend his working hours. (Aristotle's 'function of man as man' is quite distinct from the function of the lute-player or the harness-maker and does not imply it.[1]) Many people are presented with no choice at all as to what they must work at: but still they ask What is to be the point of my life? The words of Micah emphasise that what we are matters rather than what particular things we choose to do: but I suspect the particular things he had in mind were ritualistic acts and these (he is saying) are not important as compared with the quality of our lives in all their complexity. (The authentic voice of Protestantism.) But the answer is meant as an answer to a practical question: and one cannot say that it is unimportant what I do whether inside or outside my working hours. It is in these actions that the quality of my moral life is to be shown: and this is what matters to God. And if anyone says: the choice of a task (whether professional or not) is irrelevant to the quality of one's moral life, then either he means that whatever your place in life, and however you arrived there, you can still try: or else he means nonsense. So I conclude that the Protestant answer, while what it says is meant to be comprehended in the words of Micah, adds something more. The Protestant idea of a peculiar calling is that something more.

[1] *Nicomachean Ethics*, Book I, Chapter 7.

Obviously the *special-task* view will work for some and not for others. Some will feel sure that they have found their vocation: others not. If we accept only the more inward interpretation it suggests that it does not finally matter what I do but only how I live. This seems to me inadequate but may work for some people. At least the answer (phrased in the first or in the second terms) is an answer to a responsible person who wants to know what his life is given to him *for*: what is to decide for him his most fundamental aim in life. And with all its faults the answer has the great merit of being both intelligible and absolute for those who accept it. While it admits all sorts of perplexity and hesitation and failure, it altogether excludes the view that my life has no purpose, that there is no reason why I am here, that what I do does not matter.

This answer presupposes that God has *beneficent* purposes. On some views of God's nature, it may become difficult to say that what these could be. (This goes with the whole difficulty of God having aims which he brings about by his and perhaps by our labour.) The Protestant view, on the whole, means by the beneficence of God what we mean by the beneficence of man: and imagines God as loving men and looking for men's good in every way—their virtue and their happiness. Butler says that the only positive moral excellence we can clearly conceive in God is benevolence. (At this point he is regarding justice, fidelity and veracity as negative restrictions upon the workings of benevolence.)[1] In effect the Protestant answer supposes that God's aims and purposes centre on man

---

[1] *Sermons*, XII.

and his good: in the Quietist version the aim seems to be that man should do justice, love mercy and walk humbly: and this is both virtue and happiness in one. Are we to distinguish God's own inherent goodness from the goodness that is to be achieved in men? No doubt Protestant orthodoxy has always made a distinction: but at all events the goodness of God is understood as an extension and perfection of the goodness sometimes shown by men in their dealings with each other: and what God has in store for men is reward or punishment in the next life: this is God's justice. To those who repent he offers mercy. All sorts of other themes occur and had to be accommodated in Protestant theology (including much that is discussed in the second answer). I am speaking of what seems to me a mainstream of humanistic Protestantism—one which has had and still has an immense influence. It is humanistic because it centres upon goodness as men understand it and on human happiness.

The second answer does not put man in this central position. The centre is God: and his infinity of positive attributes is entirely beyond our understanding. Even God's moral goodness can be described only by analogy with what we call moral goodness. God is entirely complete and self-sufficient and cannot be said to *need* anything. He created men but he need not have done so. Why then do men exist (and why do I exist)? The answer seems to be that the redemption of sinful man is the supreme expression of God's goodness or glory. God made man to sin. Sin is unintelligible unless as a voluntary action: so then God made men to have and misuse free will. I shall not attempt to explain how Adam who was made by God came to sin: but in the divine plan this was intended:

Adae peccatum...O felix culpa!

Thereafter it is by sin and in sin that we are born and this sin is what God redeems men from. The sin is still said to be voluntary but all those who are born of the flesh are born to sin. And everyone who (by the proper procedures) repents and is redeemed, does so by God's power and to God belongs all the glory. The punishment of the unrepentant also redounds to God's glory. In a secondary sense God is concerned with man's moral goodness and happiness: they are part of what is meant by redemption. But the supreme purpose of our being here at all is not that *we* should achieve anything or enjoy anything. It is that God's glory should be completed. One facet of this is that God bestows a vision of himself on those he redeems, not normally in this life but at some time after death and purgatory. Certainly God owes us nothing: but the converse does not hold. Although we are here for God's greater glory, yet we owe him our love and gratitude for our creation and redemption.

This view provides an answer to both questions: why is there anything at all (besides God whose non-existence is inconceivable)? Why does the universe, as we (in part) know it, exist at all? God created it for his glory. Why are we here? God created us in order that he might redeem us from our sin and perhaps reveal himself to us. What are we to do with our lives? Repent and obey God.

This brings happiness in the next life and at least alleviates unhappiness in this. Fear and hope are motives for repentance. But the goodness and happiness of men is not the reason why we are here. To that question the answer is *for God's glory*. We may say that God is just and also merciful: but these attributes cannot be clearly understood by us and we have finally to admit that the world was made and we are born, for the sake of something we can never understand. Before God our first feeling ought to be one of guilt: but again this is not to be measured in ordinary human terms. The best of men is still guilty and the wisest of men will never understand (in this life) quite *how* he is guilty.

Such a view requires a sacerdotal government of our lives. We can know by the natural light what is good and what is evil and hence there is a place for reasoning about purely moral matters. But salvation does not come to the virtuous; all have sinned and divine revelation explains how God's forgiveness can be obtained. This revelation must be institutionalised. Absolution is a sacrament administered by authority: which then finally comes to direct the whole of life. Can men then after all understand? Not really. The divine revelation *tells* us many things but we are not thereby enabled to understand all that we are required to believe. However, through the Church we are at second-hand enabled to understand enough to see what God requires of us. Our aim in this life is to obey. The understanding we have of God is largely negative: we know, for example, that God is the opposite of anything evil. We have a practical understanding of what sin is, since this consists essentially in disobedience to God and to the Church. And some at least are promised a full understanding in the next life.

This answer satisfies many people: and it has long ago become evident that it is impossible (in general) to shake that satisfaction by argument. The whole position guards believers against putting their confidence in their own power of judgement: and without such confidence argument is pointless. Life may shake people into or out of such a view. I discuss it here because it has merits and because so many people have accepted it in the past and so many accept it now: and because there are people who have not lost confidence in rational argument but who are faced with a situation in which they are invited to do so. I discuss it also because those who have confidence in rational argument are under no kind of obligation to keep silence before those who have not—especially those who do so much of the talking about religion today.

That the universe exists for the glory of God is not very explicit but I think it is an answer to the first question. It turns from the universe as we know it to something which is greater, nobler, and (could we but rise to it) more intelligible, than the world we know. It states that the reason for the world cannot be found by looking here and about in the world: which is what many people are driven to conclude. It is an appeal beyond all we can know or understand in this life: to perfection negatively or abstractly described but in itself wholly positive and absolutely real.

Job was troubled about *his* existence, his life in this world. Could we say that this view answers the question: Why me? I think it does. I may be a grasshopper in God's sight but my existence is what he wills and the view prohibits us from asking whether God's glory would not have been fully expressed without my life, sin, salvation or damnation. If it is to be spelt out hesitantly, the answer will have to be that my life is what God in his perfection willed.

Does this view tell me what I ought to do with my life? Yes. I ought to repent and (following the natural light) to live virtuously: and I ought to make my peace with God by the sacraments. To this is added the hope that God will choose me for some supernatural enlightenment: and the promise that at some time after death a vision of God awaits all those who are saved. And I can know that at every stage God's dealings with me are wholly just, even if they seldom seem so to me.

It may be argued that I have not in this account done justice to the doctrine of the vision of God: that the view could more fairly be represented as an account of God's labours to share His glory with certain redeemed finite spirits—labours on men's behalf. I think many do take this view but that it places men alongside God in a manner which is repugnant to the orthodox view—the sole aim of which seems to be the exaltation of God. We have also to consider that only some spirits enjoy this vision: many are condemned to everlasting torment. This, too, is a manifestation of God's glory. And such a doctrine does not seem to me to accept the view that men are of value in themselves. One could add that the more generous tenets could be combined with the Protestant view. It is, of course, true that the first view often includes the notion of everlasting punishment, but as a matter of justice: not that God made man to glorify himself in this peculiar way.

Of course, one of the great difficulties of both views is: can you believe all this? I am not here concerned with the logical question. Certainly many do believe. The first objection I want to make against the second view is that it introduces a notion of God's glory and hence of his goodness that makes no sense at all in the moral terms we understand and employ in our secular thinking— including our thinking about such intimate and vital matters as friendship and families. To reply that the divine attributes can be understood only negatively or by analogy does not seem to me to meet the difficulty. I cannot conscientiously say that the divine work appears to me close enough to what I call goodness to merit the title of glory or goodness in an analogical sense.

Connected with this is the fact (for it seems to me to be a fact) that even the analogies by which God's moral attributes are explained are unacceptable. We are invited to think of God as an absolute ruler, a despotic father, a lover of 'justice' in a sense many people now find repugnant. 'Whom the Lord loveth he chasteneth and scourgeth every son whom he receiveth' is not an acceptable picture of a father. And those who tell me that we are all grasshoppers in his sight seem really to mean that unbelievers are grasshoppers in *their* sight. (And in any case, is this fair to grasshoppers?)

The feeling of guilt is familiar enough, but is it the one on which one would wish to construct an account of the world and of man? It encourages (as it seems to me) just the wrong kind of childishness and certainly those who are dominated by it will need to be treated as children. 'Make a person feel guilty and he will do what he is told.'[1] The uncertainty of its fundamental meaning seems to me to deprive it of the power to give a man intelligible and accepted guidance as to how he should live, what he should do with his life. Commands it will certainly give: but not a reasonable ideal or plan.

The third view holds that we are here to prepare ourselves for another life: only on this supposition can we make sense of this life. We see that childhood prepares us for grown-up life: and that as we are learning how to live, time passes and our powers begin to decline. *Si jeunesse savait: si vieillesse pouvait.* We are just learning the art when the whole process is interrupted. This can be regarded as unjust: hence we may suppose that a just God will give us an opportunity to use our powers in another life. (The notion of justice on a cosmic scale was considered in Chapter 1.) The argument from justice applies with special force to all those who see that they really have powers which some hard fate or some one weakness prevents them from exercising. It applies to those who make irrevocable choices and make them innocently but mistakenly: to those who know they will die young: to those who feel that life has been very hard

[1] Harry Williams in *Objections to Christian Belief*, p. 50.

on them *but* has taught them special lessons too late to practice them. The view is that a just God must right these individual wrongs and that it will have to be in another world—not presumably for them only, but for the species.

There is another aspect to the view which has more to do with natural economy than with justice: and which begins with man as man rather than with individual men. This is the view that death is naturally absurd: something repugnant to nature, contrary to the indications given by the stages of organic life. Since all living things complete their cycle in death this analogy is perhaps not a very strong one in logic: but has a wide appeal. The appeal must rest upon some definite thing in man's life which is *not* completed even in a full life. And I think what many have in mind is a broad moral notion of how to live. We all believe that life teaches us many things: when is this phase to be fulfilled by putting the teaching into practice? In this life obviously it often happens that there is no opportunity. It is arguable that the kind of thing our life is, is a state of learning and proving, and that the best of people go on doing this throughout life. This then is the great preparation which does not naturally stop as long as we live. Where is the stage of using and applying what we have learned?

> A senseless school where we must give
> Our lives that we may learn to live !
> A dolt is he who memorizes
> Lessons that leave no time for prizes.[1]

[1] Thomas Hardy: *Time's Laughingstocks.*

45

We can imagine such a state (it is claimed): and on the analogy of other organic processes one might expect it. Life only makes sense if we believe there is such a stage in a life to come. We may become familiar with the notion that others are cut off with their powers unused. But the idea of our own death cannot be accepted:

There is no such thing as a natural death. . . All men must die: but for every man his death is an accident and, even if he knows it and consents to it, an unjustifiable violation.[1]

If, however, this life is accepted as being an education for another, then its trials and difficulties make a kind of sense. A bold statement of this view is given by the Grammarian 'shortly after the revival of learning in Europe': 'Now master, take a little rest' excites from him the rebuke: 'Leave *now* for dogs and apes: man has forever.'[2] Of him it is only a *verbal* paradox to say that 'before living he'd learn how to live'. Of course, this view is supernatural in a sense: it is certainly humanistic and humane: it enlists all men in an extensive educational project for their own benefit. If the appeal is to justice rather than to perfection (or economy), then I think the view must be theistic: it makes an appeal to the notion of what is fair—especially what is a fair opportunity or a fair reward: it need not involve the notion of punishment. I think it makes a wide appeal and that there are many people who could hardly bear to go on living unless they believed in it.

Clearly some form of this view is usually a part of the

[1] Simone de Beauvoir.
[2] Robert Browning: 'A Grammarian's Funeral'.

first view: and with many reservations, something like it appears also in the second view. Nevertheless, it is worth considering by itself because to many people, whatever else they may believe or think they believe, the answer to the second question is to be found in the notion of an after-life which alone can make sense of this life.

It is easy to see that the mere notion of another life is not enough. Because this other life might not in any way explain this life: and it might itself need further explanation. Some people do, of course, hold that we are living out a series of lives: but then for them the sense of this whole series is to be looked for in some different stage or plane of existence altogether. The argument I wish to consider is that the nature of our present life requires that there should be another life which explains this one. And hints of such a view are to be found in many religions and philosophies. To meet the requirement, the second life must be different from the first: or at least the two lives taken together must be different from this life considered alone. The second life must compensate for the injustice of this life: or must complement its incompleteness: or both. And it must do this in a way which does not itself require another life in order to explain the inadequacies or unfairnesses of the two lives taken together. If we were given an opportunity in another life to act out what we had learned in this life, then as that life progressed we must be able to see that our whole existence taken together makes sense: it is just or perfect in a way in which life as we now know it is not. How this can be, may be something we do not understand clearly. For most people it is enough to have an expectation or even a hope that there will be justice and perfection in another life.

Are we to expect then that we die not once but twice: that the second life will be long enough to perfect the first and that will be all? This is not what believers in an after-life seem to have in mind. If we are saying that man must achieve a certain perfection: or achieve a certain happiness by his efforts in this life or the next, it is tempting to think that this means that we die once and then begin an after-life which has no end. Two arguments might be said to support this view.

First, the ideal of happiness seems to require *unending* happiness. Kant said that although all the elements of our notion of happiness are derived from experience, yet the notion 'requires an absolute whole, a maximum of welfare in my present and all future circumstances'.[1] The argument in terms of justice would be that the righteous deserve happiness and this means an infinite. It is rather a precarious argument: happiness has to be thought of, as theologians thought of freedom of the will, as meaningless if it is not unlimited. Or that a just God could never destroy a virtuous soul? And perhaps, if given time, every soul can become righteous and so deserve unending happiness.

Secondly, in terms of perfection the argument must be that the new life somehow lies outside time altogether, and so avoids the paradoxical incompleteness of this life.

[1] *Fundamental Principles of the Metaphysic of Ethics*, p. 42.

In the next life I apply the lessons I have learned in this life; but as long as I go on living and suffering in time, I shall go on learning: and this gives rise to the same sort of problem. For the more I learn the less time I have to work out what I learn. For this reason, amongst many others, the new life is thought of as on a different plane from this one. Aristotle in the last book of his *Ethics* argues that it is all very well to find out, but it is a higher thing altogether to enjoy what has been found out. Contemplation might be compared with a state in which we know and have nothing more to come to know. For his part Aristotle was prepared to admit that the theoretic life includes both learning and contemplating: and that it is in fact interrupted by other demands and by weariness and that it ends in death. (What it means for God is another matter.) But the notion of just *enjoying* may do something to clarify the view that another life cannot bring us to perfection if it is a life lived in the changes and chances of time. Therefore it must somehow be outside time altogether: being, not doing.

This more sophisticated argument from perfection probably counts little with most people. What they mostly want is a further chance, a new deal, a fresh start.

I have not examined the logical cogency of these arguments from justice (divine justice) or from perfection (which could simply be natural and human perfection). Nor have I asked what kind of sense it makes to speak of a person continuing after the death of his body; or of a person as having life outside time altogether. All I wish to establish is that the view is designed to produce an answer to the questions: Why are we all here? Why am I here? And that the answer cannot be (and need not be) a detailed one. It must be in very general terms and the future life must be thought of as different from this one: perhaps a quite different mode of being altogether.

Therefore, death remains a portentous landmark and a great division between souls. From our side little is known; imagination falters. To believe firmly in such another life by no means prevents us from mourning the death of others and (in a sense) mourning our own death. That there is this barrier is seen very clearly in the burial service of the Book of Common Prayer. Only spiritualism seems to try to ignore the great gap which it is surely very natural to feel between the living and the dead.

CHAPTER 3

A METAPHYSICAL ANSWER

<><><><><><><><><><><><><><><><><><><><><><><><><><><><>

ONE NOTION OF 'another world than ours' suggests that there is a paradoxical feature of the practical life which is lived through: that as we live we learn and the longer we live the more we know and the less time we have for practising what we have learned. Partly for this reason Aristotle finally (and rather unexpectedly) decides that the best life, the most perfect life, is the theoretic life in which we are engaged in contemplating what we know. This is the only kind of life we can ascribe to the gods: and (he says) the nearer we are to achieving it the nearer we come to happiness.[1]

In this chapter I wish to examine the notion that what gives final point to life is not any kind of practical aim or achievement, but knowing and understanding and contemplating the truth. It will be an important question what exactly is included in 'the truth' here. But the point of this doctrine is that it sets up the ideal of a life wholly ruled by reason: and this means a life freed from the interruptions, compromises, and diversions which characterise the life of practical achievement. The theoretic life aims at understanding, not altering, mastering, or improving the world. The view is that some things at least can be perfectly understood: all things can be *judged*

[1] Aristotle, *Nicomachean Ethics*, Book x, Chapter 7 etc.

in a purely rational way. But no pursuit which has a practical aim can be wholly reasonable.

To decide that what I am here for is to know and understand the world is to come very near to identifying a man with his reason. 'The mind of anyone is that person': 'A man is what he knows.' What then is he to *do*? To reason, know, understand. It is important to notice that this is a decision about life: and in favour of *an activity* (for knowing and even contemplating what we know is an activity) and that it places other activities lower down in the scale of importance. The activity placed first—and which may be held to be what alone makes life worth having—is not one which adds anything to the world or takes anything away.

It may also provide an answer to the first question. The world in which we are set is a world of change and chance in which nothing is ever perfected, nothing permanent, nothing secure. But this world can be understood: through the changes of this world we can come to know truths, such as the principles of mathematics, which are timeless. The world as we experience it may be held to exist for the sake of leading minds towards what is permanent, changeless and perfect in itself.

I shall consider two views of the theoretic life: these are (to give them labels) the Rationalist view and the Empiricist view. The first, and more ambitious view holds two things to be true: (i) That all that can be known is in principle capable of being understood as rational— that there is a necessary reason why the truths of science are as they are; that all that can be known by us is part of a single system all of whose connexions are necessary: hence that there are necessary truths of fact or existence. And (ii) That while we can never know or understand all this by our minds in this life, there is to be a complete knowledge somewhere—if not by us then by the mind of God of which our minds are fragmentary copies or parts. The Rationalist view is found in some of the works of Plato and Aristotle: and in the medieval philosophers and in the Rationalists of the Renaissance and the Enlightenment—Descartes, Leibniz, Spinoza: it was revived with a new logic by Hegel and the Romantics. It is an important point about the Rationalist view that it offers an answer to both questions. It answers the second question: What am I here for? in the sense of to serve what end, for what purpose? The answer is: To know, to understand. The Rationalist view also answers the question in the sense of suggesting *how it came about* that I am here. My existence is a matter of fact but it cannot be accidental—since there must be a sufficient reason for ordinary matters of fact as well as for mathematical truths. Not only can I (in principle) come to know how the world works: I can also know that there is some necessary and sufficient reason why it works as it does— a fully satisfying explanation, one which is (to a rational mind) decisive and compelling. But this kind of ex- planation of the cause of any particular existence—myself or any other—cannot be based upon part-knowledge of the world. All matters of fact are connected. Hence this view offers an answer to the first question: Why is everything here? Why is anything here? And this must answer the question: Why am I here? The answer must be logically satisfactory, compelling, unquestionable.

Nevertheless Leibniz retains a distinction between truths of reason (logic and pure mathematics) and truths of fact—what is the case but could be conceived not to be the case. That twice two makes four is a truth of reason: we cannot conceive that it should be otherwise. That Adam sinned is a truth of fact: we can quite well re-write the story of the Garden of Eden imagining Adam to have rejected the temptation to sin. The Rationalists saw that we are obliged to rely on our senses and our memories and on testimony for our beliefs about matters of fact: and many of these beliefs are not held with certainty. However they held out a kind of promise: If our minds were only comprehensive enough then we should find a logically decisive reason for every *truth* of fact.

Of course Leibniz and Spinoza did not promise such knowledge to everyone or about everything. They contrasted what is infinitely complicated with what is only finitely complicated. Knowledge of infinities is not normally possible for finite minds: although we can understand in a general way what it is for a matter to be infinitely complex; and see in a general way that a given matter must be infinitely complex. It will be agreed that we can understand that between any two real numbers there is another real number; hence that the stretch of real numbers between any pair must be infinite. What is comprised in such a stretch, no finite mind can grasp in detail. The Rationalists hold that there are actual infinities: whether parts of wholes, or members of collections, or successive members in causal series. Hence the detailed causal explanation of existing things would be infinitely complex and beyond the normal powers of a finite mind. But we can understand that there *is* such an explanation and that it is infinitely complex. To this may be added the view that God understands the whole: perhaps that we may understand in another life: or that there is some special kind of knowledge which is attained sometimes by some people: and that those who attain it do comprehend the full reason for the existence of something—for example, of their own selves or minds.[1]

Such extraordinary knowledge would meet the objection of one who says: I cannot see that the existence and union of my parents explains my existence. He is unwilling to accept the working principles of the world as good enough. He is unwilling to accept general laws (which are only summary descriptions of the world as a going concern) as being really compelling *reasons*. The Rationalist cannot deal with this difficulty by offering to *demonstrate* the laws of nature or to show how from such laws my existence necessarily follows. Rationalists of course know that this cannot be done in detail. But they hold that we can know certain principles about the world: and from these we can understand that there must be a compelling reason and that it must be infinitely complex. What are these principles which we can know? The different philosophers have offered different principles. They might be described as the principles of

[1] For example Spinoza's 'Third kind of knowledge', *Ethics*, v.

cosmic economy: that everything existing has a cause: that for everything that does not exist there is a cause why it does not exist: that there are no two existents perfectly alike; that there are no real gaps, everything that is (in some sense) possible being somewhere actual. And so on.

If something of the sort were true, would it make our knowledge of the world as satisfactory to the mind as our knowledge of mathematics? We have to distinguish between general laws of change and descriptions of particular situations. When we have a notion of the general laws of change we can predict what will be the state of a certain field at a given time in the future: and we can (working backwards) explain what previously existing state must have given rise to the field as it is at present. This is how causal arguments are explored *in limited fields*. But one premise of any such argument is a description of the field at a certain time. What kind of description would it be which gave the distribution of the forces and which also was itself intellectually convincing, necessary, unavoidable? Two lines of argument can be detected. One shows that a given state of affairs *must* result from general laws operating (perhaps over an infinite period of time) on a random field. This seems to say: we can demonstrate that a given arrangement must result from a previous arrangement which *could be anything*. So that we seem to explain an arrangement at a given time without making any supposition about the character of the original arrangement. The Greek Atomists used this method in their accounts of the origin of the world. But it seems that to say the original field was 'random' is not the same thing as to say that no particular supposition is made about it—that it could be anything. Certain possible original arrangements would exclude certain results; to explain a given field therefore it must be assumed that the original arrangement was not one of these. Why not? And finally it is far from clear what a random arrangement is. So that there is considerable doubt whether this kind of explanation ever works.

The other kind of argument will be that the original arrangement *must have* certain properties. For example: Nothing possible must be omitted: it *must be* complete. Arguments of this sort are offered in terms too general to produce strong conviction. Again the meaning of 'complete' is far from clear. This is the type of argument much used by Spinoza and Leibniz. As the notion of infinitely 'complex' is (to our minds) intelligible only in pure mathematics, so also the notion of an arrangement that is intellectually satisfying and compelling derives from the same source. The arrangement of numbers in series is an intellectually satisfying one. Five by its very nature must be 'placed' between 4 and 6. It would be a long story to explain why this order is so convincing: but surely an element that is purely conventional enters into the explanation. (It is convincing because we made the arrangement—we all agreed to it.) Again the notion of 'completeness' makes sense in respect of numbers: the series of cardinal integers 4 5 6 completes a stretch and nothing *can* be added or removed between 4 and 6. But it seems doubtful whether the numbers provide a good analogy for explaining the incidence of existing things. Leibniz thought so but Leibniz never gets beyond very general applications.[1]

Suppose the Rationalist arguments were acceptable, would they really answer the questions: Why does the world exist? Why does it include me? Clearly they give an answer to both: and there are grave objections to be made against the two answers. There is a further difficulty (which Leibniz discussed) in the answer to the second question. The Rationalists' explanation of my existence must be that it is not in itself necessary. Only God's existence is so. But my existence is necessary to *a whole* which has to exist because God wills it and because it is perfect or in some way inevitable. I have to exist in somewhat the same way as the number 5 has to exist. But of course this means that I have to have a certain character: just as the number 5 has to be greater than 4 and has to be prime. On this view I am not asked to accept, as a final and sufficient reason for my existence, the fact that my parents existed and produced me according to the laws of nature which happen to hold. I am asked to believe that this came about because the perfection and therefore the existence of the universe required a certain arrangement and certain laws. Some find this satisfactory: but it is not clear that it can explain me as a free agent. Here of course it has to be admitted that the notion of a free agent is very far from clear. But at least the number 5 is not helpful: it certainly cannot be what it pleases. It may

[1] Leibniz, *Monadology*.

be that those who claim to be free agents cannot logically also ask for a necessary reason why they exist. Leibniz does offer a round-about explanation in theological terms.[1] Kant, who was familiar with this explanation, thought that the very notion of an explanation of freedom as a part of nature was absurd. If Kant is right, then either I am not after all a free agent, or the Rationalist explanation fails.

Again, suppose the Rationalist view were acceptable: does this support the ideal of the purely intellectual life? Of course the connexion is not absolutely binding. It is possible to accept the Rationalist view of nature and hold that what man is here for is to pursue some practical aim —or even simply to idle along enjoying what he can. But at all events it very greatly strengthens the view that we are here to know and understand. For on this view the scope of what we can know and understand is indefinitely extended. There is nothing really unintelligible in the universe. 'There is nothing waste, nothing sterile, nothing dead in the universe, no chaos, no confusion, save in appearance.'[2] 'The mind of a man *is* the man.' If reason is man's essence, then we may well conclude that he is here to know and to understand. This was the view of Spinoza and Leibniz, although both go on to relate the life of reason to the life of practical pursuits.

Aristotle did so by maintaining that even the philosopher must live in the world and therefore must take some part in its practical affairs. The philosopher is not a god.

[1] See Chapter 2, pp. 38–9; Kant, *Fundamental Principles of the Metaphysic of Ethics*, §3, p. 95 etc.   [2] Leibniz, *Monadology*, § 69.

The life of practice must in any case be the only life open to many men: and a man shows his reason not only in the intellectual virtues but also in the moral virtues. The distinction between theoretical and practical is not obscured: and the highest place is given to the theoretical. The later Rationalists tried to find a subtler and closer relationship between discovering, knowing, understanding what there is, and leading a good life—making the right decisions in practical affairs and carrying them out. They held that the object of pure knowledge is reality and that reality is in itself perfect. What falls short of knowledge has something less than reality as its object: but if there is an object at all it must have some degree of reality (less than is generally supposed perhaps) and therefore some degree of perfection. But practical virtue is a disposition to act well, to do what is good or perfect. Knowledge of reality or perfection is therefore a necessary condition of living well: and a sufficient condition of knowing how to live well. Are we then to leave a gap between knowing what the good is and actually doing what is good? There is a way of closing this gap also. It was the opinion of Socrates that a man always acts as he believes it best: he fails to do what is best only where he is ignorant of what it is.[1] This intellectualises the will: and this is a characteristic Rationalist doctrine. From all which it would seem to follow that in pursuing truth for its own sake we come to know and to do the good: with whatever degree of success. And the

[1] See Plato's *Protagoras* and Aristotle's *Nicomachean Ethics*, Book VII, Chapter 2.

great distinction of intellectual–practical gives place to a new distinction between what is real, understood and enacted on the one hand, and on the other what is mere appearance, confusedly known and imperfectly carried out.

This scheme is vulnerable at two important points. How does a notion of perfection give rise to notions of moral conduct? How does it ever enable us to work out a question of practical importance?—Which would be right? Which should I do? Kant says that the notion of perfection in this very wide metaphysical sense is too general, too vague, and in itself has no moral content. If we are able from some other source to frame a notion of morality we may include this under the general name of perfection. But then we do not really employ this general notion in guiding our conduct: for morality comes to us from another source. Kant divides Pure and Practical Reason: and perfection is a concept of Pure Reason to which morality (a concept of Practical Reason) can without manifest contradiction be *added*. Kant also argues that *what is the case*, however clearly and distinctly it is understood, cannot decide for us the practical question: What ought to be?[1]

The second vulnerable point is of course the opinion of Socrates, that a man always acts as he believes to be best. Aristotle says this 'seems to conflict with the facts'. What

[1] Kant, *Fundamental Principles of the Metaphysic of Ethics*, §2, p. 74. It is Kant who most firmly rejects the Aristotelian view that the theoretical reason is supreme. His reasons for taking this stand are analysed and critically discussed in Mr G. J. Warnock's British Academy Lecture, 'The primacy of Practical Reason', 1966.

facts? Many would say that we are very familiar with situations in which we contemplate a move required by a rule which we have been following. And we break the rule. This clearly happens in many non-moral contexts where the rules are provided by tradition, games, legislation, etc. Many philosophers still hold the opinion of Socrates: that in all such cases the rule we know, while it provides us with a reason for doing a certain action, does not provide us with a final and sufficient reason. We break the rule but for a reason—some *other* reason. In cases where a moral issue is involved and I have always professed a certain principle—how can I go against it? The answer given is: Some hitherto neglected moral aspect of the case comes to my notice and I modify my rule to cover the new case. But is the reason necessarily of the form: 'It would be better to go against the rule': and what does 'better' mean here? Is this itself a moral move? The opinion of Socrates is that it is—although it may look strange and even repugnant. But such a view is very difficult to reconcile with a Rationalist view of right and wrong. According to the Rationalist view, we can *know* right and wrong. The opinion of Socrates is now embraced chiefly by those who hold a quite different view of right and wrong. This conflicts with the Rationalist view of reality, perfection, knowledge of right and wrong—and action in the light of pure reason. While I do not pretend to settle any of these views, I think it is fair to say that the argument of the Rationalists is vulnerable at this stage.[1]

[1] See also Chapter 7, pp. 164–7.

There is a second view of what the theoretic life consists in: the view of the Empirical philosophers, Locke, Hume, Mill, and of Kant.

The claims of the Rationalists have been rejected by Kant, by the Empiricists and by the analytical philosophers of more recent times. First it is absolutely denied that any truths about what actually exists can be seen to be necessary. This makes a very sharp distinction between logic and mathematics on the one hand and all other knowledge—scientific, historical etc. Secondly, our knowledge of logic and mathematics has been questioned: Is 'the hardness of the logical *must*' (in 2 × 2 must equal 4) derived in the end from familiarity with conventional rules and the modes of their application?[1] Is this 'must' the same as we find in a game—where the rules are simply traditional or even made up by ourselves? Do the propositions of mathematics state anything or state nothing? Thirdly, the whole Rationalist conception of being has been challenged: the Rationalist deals in the general kinds of things, 'essences'; and for him 'to be' is to be an instance of some general characteristic or set of characteristics. Leibniz's notion of an individual is that of the sole instance of an infinitely complex set of characteristics. The Existentialists argue that this is an inadequate, misleading and mischievous notion: and in particular that it fails to give any account of the being of a person who can choose what to do and hence choose what character he is to have.

But in spite of the general retreat from Rationalism,[1]

[1] Wittgenstein, *Philosophical Investigations*, Part I, §437.

the attraction of the theoretic life has not seriously diminished except perhaps for the Existentialists.

What is the peculiar charm of the theoretic life? All practical pursuits require us to try to understand and know certain things—to answer certain questions about the world. But it is life that presents us with the questions we have to answer: we do not choose them for ourselves. And we have to offer an answer within a given time whether we have adequate grounds or not. To some it seems beneath the dignity of rational beings to be forced to answer questions when they know they have not examined all the evidence or weighed all the probabilities. And there is always this *model* by which we can (if we so decide) condemn the life of practical activity. In purely theoretical enquiries we choose our own problems and never need feel compelled to answer them until we are ready to do so. It is commonly held that in mathematics we can sometimes give a final answer to a question of our choosing. We are *driven to a conclusion*. And this is not a restriction upon our intellectual freedom but the exercise of the greatest freedom we have. (Nothing can shake our conviction.) Reasons may absolutely convince us: the question is answered. We may come to the conclusion that we *know* very little: but it remains one of the wonderful facts of life that, in mathematics if nowhere else, we can construct a real proof. To do this we need something more than ambition and cleverness: we need candour as well as clarity of mind: the willingness to acknowledge what we see to be the case however much we may wish it were not. These are important faculties, important virtues: and in mathematics they are seen to have application.

> Too often it is said that there is no absolute truth, but only opinion and private judgement; that each of us is conditioned, in his view of the world, by his own peculiarities, his own taste and bias; that there is no external kingdom of truth to which, by patience, by discipline, we may at last obtain admittance, but only truth for me, for you, for every separate person. By this habit of mind one of the chief ends of human effort is denied, and the supreme virtue of candour, of fearless acknowledgement of what is, disappears from our moral vision. Of such scepticism mathematics is a perpetual reproof; for its edifice of truths stands unshakable and inexpugnable to all the weapons of doubting cynicism.[1]

These are the words of Bertrand Russell writing sixty years ago. Today this claim even for mathematics would be rejected by many philosophers; but what they would substitute for it is a claim which I think most people would still regard as a claim to *knowledge*. It is now generally agreed that our beliefs about the physical world (about things that actually exist) are not final: but here too what is said may be given every reasonable qualification and so may be counted as a reasonable statement. And sometimes we can offer answers to questions in the empirical sciences which close the matter for the time being: which may be accepted for a generation. And we also feel free at all times to decline to answer a question: to postpone it, to leave it alone or leave it to others.

The theoretic life is not seriously disturbed by the

[1] Russell, *Philosophical Essays*, 1910, p. 85.

thought that I myself shall never know how long my work has stood: or what superseded it. Just as I have inherited the work of others, so let others inherit mine. The theoretic life is a conversation of fellow-workers who may belong to the same or to different ages. Knowledge (mathematical, scientific, historical) is both cumulative and impersonal.

In the fields of morals and politics and the arts, the belief that progress is inevitable is thoroughly discredited. But in knowledge there is progress and while this can be stopped or reversed from *outside*, the nature of enquiry is such that if left to itself it grows from strength to strength. Those who devote their lives to theoretical enquiries can feel that they are part of an activity that is inexhaustible and yet always progressing. This holds in the realm of necessary truth and of contingent truth. What constitutes progress is not practical success: the criteria are rational and autonomous. Of course much theoretical activity is very largely wasted because redundant or trivial. The test as to whether a piece of work is redundant is unfortunately not an internal test: it depends upon communication as well as on logic. (That two people are setting themselves the same question is of course a matter of logic. That one continues his enquiry in ignorance of the other is commonly a matter of accident.) That a line of enquiry 'leads nowhere' does not usually mean that it was a waste of effort: the effort has proved a negative. The tests of importance are internal. I have said that one of the chief attractions of the theoretic life is that we choose our own questions. But in fact 'we' here means 'those interested and competent': they judge the way an enquiry is going and frame the next questions of importance for that enquiry. The clearer the indications the better. One might say that a scientist or historian found himself 'compelled' to try to answer a certain question. But this is logical compulsion: he is guided by the same sort of considerations as a man who is 'driven to a conclusion'. This is freedom. This is how, in the theoretic life, we choose our questions. Of course where a man is compelled in this way he may still be in error. Even where all are agreed in accepting an answer as logically cogent, all may be mistaken. This possibility is built into the very logic we apply. We have nothing else to rely on but the consensus of competent opinion. Any one who thinks this is a regrettable defect should ask himself just what he has in mind when he thinks of some other way of settling a question. Whatever method he proposes must first of all be accepted as rational: that is, accepted by the consensus of competent opinion.

Knowledge is also in a sense impersonal. It cannot be private to me or to any individual. It must be something done together. Of course only people can do mathematics or study physics or history: only people can try to understand. But if I claim to know or to understand I make a claim on behalf of all rational beings. It is also true that only rational beings and some other animals can perceive physical objects. But that does not make what they perceive private or individual to them. There could not be a private physical object: any object that I see could exist without my seeing it; could be perceived by others or by no one. So also there cannot be a private mathematics or physics or history. And it is easy to see that knowledge, just because it is not private or individual, does to some degree transcend the limitations of our ordinary lives. One might feel this in trying to follow a proof constructed by someone in Ancient Greece: for example the proof that there is no highest prime number. And a man might have the ambition to construct a proof that should last as long a time. So it happens that in every civilised country there have been men and (in modern times) women whose great purpose in life could be simply stated: to add to human knowledge or to preserve and transmit it, or both. This has seemed to give a point to the individual's life, a purpose which makes life worth while. It is of all things we do the least personal, the least individual: and this for some people is itself a great attraction. Knowledge is speech at its most impersonal, its most objective. Man can face up to the truth; he can try to empty himself of all his preconceptions and see things—some things—as they are. In this way he comes to know a world which transcends the limitations of his own life. This is the great attraction of the theoretic life. And the question is: can this be accepted as an answer to the second question: Why am I here? What am I to live for? To know (in part), to understand (in part).

This view of knowledge seems to leave something out. The fundamental sciences require great devotion to the internal requirements of the system: it is by reference to the system that we come to an understanding of the world. And it is for many of the greatest minds a wholly satisfactory limitation: to examine and explain matter, or living matter, or a certain group of substances. But that this provides a full-time occupation, a life-time of devotion for some, does not in itself indicate that the purpose or meaning of our life is to know and understand. A chemist does not really believe that the aim of our life is to understand chemical compounds: he knows that this is really only a branch of physics: and on the other hand that certain developments in chemistry are important for biological rather than chemical reasons. Yet chemistry is a whole-time occupation—even one sub-branch of chemistry. The special sciences inevitably consider each other. But many of them also consider technology: and what is done or aimed at in technology depends on the needs and aims of mankind. The mere fact that a science (or even all the sciences taken together) have autonomous tests of validity and importance (i.e. of what it is to understand the world) is enough to make them worth pursuing for their own sakes: but does nothing to contradict the view that they are also (in varying degrees) studied (and properly studied) in order to enable men to control the external world and even themselves. The view that knowledge alone constitutes the aim of man seems to be partial, abstract, withdrawn.

In this connexion it is important to compare the arts—poetry, music, painting and sculpture. These too are often represented as having their own tests of validity, their own notion of system, their own sense of direction. And it is certainly claimed that they are worth pursuing entirely for their own sakes: and sometimes that it is in the arts that we find the real and true purpose or end of human life.

It is clear that in many ways the practice of the arts (and the life that it requires) is analogous with the practice of knowing and understanding: and it is a remarkable fact that Aristotle makes no mention of them in his account of the theoretic life. What are the likenesses: and what are the differences which may have led Aristotle to exclude the arts?

We may say of a poet that he does not directly deal with practical questions: like the scientist, he deals in 'theory'. He chooses his theme, it is not forced upon him by circumstances as immediately practical questions are. He deals with it according to the canons of his art: and if he does not like the result he can turn to a different theme. We can of course say that what is important, even what sort of thing is to be tackled next, is determined by the progress of the art itself. Some writers seem to be irrelevant in their day who might have been relevant in a different stage of the art. This 'determination', however, is not to be regarded as a limitation upon the autonomy of the art: the consideration which makes a work important, which marks progress or new achievement, can be represented as internal. The poet is driven to write in somewhat the same way as a scientist is driven to tackle 'the next problem': and although this is altogether looser than the sense in which a mathematician who has chosen a problem is driven to accept a certain conclusion, yet as we have seen there is an analogy. So far as the governing considerations belong to the arts or to the sciences, they are what we mean by autonomy: independence of what we would *like* to see as a solution, independence of what the world would like to see as a solution.

So far the parallel goes. But there are obvious differences. First, the poet, musician or painter sets out to *make* something. He makes an arrangement of words or notes or colours: and in doing so he makes some sort of symbol. So that he may be said to have as his aim to add something new to the world. This contrasts with what the scientist or the historian does. Of course he also makes a book and perhaps makes new and subtle instruments: but these are solely for use: they are only means he has to adopt for his end—which is not to change but to understand the world. The notion that making things is somehow of a lower grade in the human scale than understanding things, is intermittently present in the Greeks and in the later Rationalists. In the sciences proper, the making is merely secondary and is often something the technician does to order. In the arts this is obviously not so. The thing made by the poet or the painter is not made merely for use: it is there to be enjoyed. Would it be fair to say that it is made merely for entertainment or diversion? Is it possible that Aristotle is hinting at this when he dismisses the notion that the good for man could consist in amusements?[1]

Of course a work of art is there to be contemplated, enjoyed—and understood—in its own right. But we nevertheless draw a fairly firm distinction between art

[1] Aristotle, *Nicomachean Ethics*, Book x, Chapter 6.

and entertainment. And such difference is not to be found simply within the structure of the work itself. It is an *indication* of the difference, that the structure is much more rudimentary in entertainment: and degrees of complexity also in some connexions indicate different degrees of importance amongst works of art themselves. But 'importance' in the arts, and also in science, is predicated on other grounds too. Some things are simple but basic; others simple and derivative: some complex and important, others complex and trivial. And in these judgements there enters something that is not to be stated simply in the canons of any one art. This is the impact of the work on human life, and especially on man's idea of himself. Here 'entertainment'—if it is really no more—offers nothing.

The validity and direction I have been considering have meaning within a given school of art or movement in art. They are often the basis of current controversies in the arts. Later generations can understand these things and may well formulate them far better than the protagonists of the time have done. But we do not now value the poetry and music and painting of the past simply in the terms of their own day. Of course any work of art from the past may have some historical interest: but what now leads us to remember and regard certain great works of art is not their place in the system or movements of their day. It is their revelation of man: the way they affect our view as to what human nature is. And looking back we see that at all stages works of art are not judged solely by internal criteria: they are recognised in their own time as important by considerations that are, in a wide sense, moral. And the internal criteria themselves connect with wider notions about how men ought to live, as well as of how men ought to paint or to write.

In the case of the arts, then, the tests of what is valid or important, the notion of the direction an art must now take, these are not explicable wholly in terms of the art itself. And the wider considerations that enter involve views about how man ought to live, about the aim and purpose or meaning of life.

But something can also be said about the sciences. Here there is a test of validity, of importance, a sense of direction, that is entirely systematic or autonomous. We can understand what science is without acknowledging that it contributes to human survival and welfare. But to regard knowledge for its own sake alone, as the purpose of man, one must weigh it against other possible purposes—the relief of suffering for example. And when we do this we see that part of the importance of science is precisely that it may contribute to the relief of suffering. But more than that, the scientist or mathematician not only practises his enquiries: he also reflects on man as a being capable of objective dispassionate enquiry. Part of the importance of science is the light in which it presents us to ourselves.

Clearly knowledge considered in abstraction can make out a claim to be pursued for its own sake. Nothing that is pursued merely *as an instrument* could in itself be said to 'give a meaning to life'. But can one say of knowledge or of the arts or both together that they alone show one the point of it all, why it is worth while being here, why one would not have missed the party?

To say this, as I have suggested and shall try to show, is to make a *practical* decision. This is a point of some interest. It is not a decision I should make. I do not believe that the Tree of Knowledge is itself the Tree of Life: that the mind of a man *is* that man. Nor do I believe that the imagination of a man considered in abstraction *is* that man: I do not believe imagination can be understood as such an abstraction. Both abstract views overlook something which seems to me essential to the notion of a person. That is his individual responsibility for what he *does*, for the practical decisions he makes and the efforts he puts into their execution: not for the final success or failure. Knowledge and art exist in a world where men are active and where men are forever changing the world: and our view of science and art is incomplete if we ignore this. To decide what is the meaning of life without considering practical questions seems to me to be opting for an ivory tower. I do not mean for an easy life: but for an incomplete one.

In the Byzantium poems, W. B. Yeats described a life at once theoretic and aesthetic. It is a life of discussion and contemplation: it deals with what is changeless and fully intelligible. It is an artificial world, as Yeats acknowledges in his image of the soul as a mechanical bird, not a 'natural thing':

> —such a form as Grecian goldsmiths make
> Of hammered gold and gold enamelling.[1]

One cannot despise such a life. But need one choose it?

[1] From *The Tower*, 1928.

CHAPTER 4

SOME INFORMAL ANSWERS

IN THIS CHAPTER I shall consider certain common-sensical answers which might be given in a candid moment to the question: Why am I here? What am I to live for? What is the point of my life? There are people whose lives seem to have a focus and who can tell us in simple and quite unsystematic terms what that focus is. And there are people who live as if their lives had a point and purpose but who might be unable to put anything into words; or who, if asked, would give a conventional answer—the answer they expect to be given to such questions, but not (for them) the answer that seems to fit. We have also to reckon with those who, 'conscious of their own ignorance, admire those who proclaim some great ideal that is above their comprehension'.[1] For the inarticulate (and either of these groups might be called inarticulate since they cannot give the true answer) we have to decide by the way they live. Thus a priest must say that the point of life is to glorify God although the point of his life seems to be to govern the Church or even his parish: and a woman might say that the point of life is to do what good one can, when in fact one would say that she lived solely for her family. I shall be interested, not in the conventional answer, but in the candid answer, and in

[1] Aristotle: *Nicomachean Ethics*, Book I, Chapter 4.

the constructions we find we can honestly put on the lives of people we know well.

The answers I shall consider do not come from authorities or pundits—although they may be used by authorities in propaganda for their own ends. They are the answers that ordinary people would give if asked about their own lives. They have a bearing on the second question rather than the first. In most cases they are so unsystematic that they imply no particular answer to the first question (about the world). It might indeed be asked whether they are really answers to the second question: Why am I here? What is my life for? Because what they really seem to do is to express a sentiment, a choice, a resolution. In effect they say: This is what I find most worthwhile in life and it is for this that I plan my life. The people who would (if candid and reflective) make such avowals, might be puzzled by the further question: Are you sure you are not mistaken? Are you sure you have found the *correct* answer? This reflection might seem beside the point: perhaps unanswerable.[1]

What may a man live by? One answer is: His work. Of course this can be fitted into the first of the theological views discussed in Chapter 2. But many who seem to find their end and aim in their work would not pay more than lip-service to these systematic notions—or would flatly reject them. John Stuart Mill, for example, said of his *System of Logic* that it was the book that 'it was in my fate to write'. And his personal letters show that he thought

[1] See also Chapter 1, pp. 13–17.

seriously of this book as the great thing in his life which gave it point and justification. He did not ask whether it was worth while: and if he had asked he would have been sure that it was. When he had finished it he was somewhat at a loss: but soon found further applications of its principles (and other projects) to occupy him. But I think he correctly believed that he had completed the work which was set for him to do. Not by God, but by circumstance.

Mill would certainly not have attempted to build on this statement. It can be that a man finds the point of his life in his work: many do not. These things happen: there is no plan. For many people there is no choice of worthwhile work; for many no choice; and for some no work. Could it be argued that provided a man has work to do (and in general man *has* to work) this can be self-justifying, can give meaning to his life? Does work in itself, no matter of what sort, give direction to life? I think some people believe that it does. Is a man not better off with work to do than without it? Most people believe so, but no doubt for many different reasons: and it is significant that one reason quite often given is: it keeps you from thinking.

To contemplate work as the focus, we must consider those who work and fail as well as those who work and succeed. And surely some kinds of work are much more satisfying than others? What makes this so? And here we soon bring in considerations that are beyond the work. What is it in aid of? What does it do to me? What does it do for other people? Some work gets excellent answers: but the answers take us beyond the work itself.

The truth seems to be that work is normally a necessary ingredient of a meaningful existence, but has to be seen in its context. In some cases the work is a means to some other end or mission and one could not be said to find the point of life in such a mission unless one worked for it as opportunity arose. Not to work would contradict the statement that one had such a mission. But of all able-bodied people living in a society, work is necessarily demanded. And that is why the deliberate choice not to work is itself a renunciation of the society in which one lives: and not to have work to do counts for many people as a rejection by their society.

If life has an end a man will want his work to contribute somehow to that end. For many people it is not enough to be able to use their leisure for the pursuit of their end or mission: they want their whole life to contribute also: and a pointless job seems to deprive life of meaning. But to have point, is it not enough that the work should be seen to be *necessary*? If the work in a university cannot go on without the cataloguing of books, does not this give point to the work of a cataloguer? If life in cities cannot go on without detergents, is there not point in filling packets with detergents? Neither worker would say that he was put into the world to do this particular job: but to do some necessary job and this is one. Necessary to what? In general terms, work is necessary for man to survive: much work is necessary for man to survive in society: to survive in a technological age: to pursue the arts and sciences, to pursue social aims. For some people, work brings a great bonus: the exercise and perfection of their own skills, plans, ideals. This is not given to many. In primitive societies at least *the necessity* of work is obvious: in technological societies it often is not. And those who have the dullest jobs may find it impossible to understand why they need to be done at all. And of course there are people of very lively mind who do not share the social aims, who feel alienated and who can be led to make the great contracting-out—by idleness, crime or suicide.

If work is taken to mean earning a living then it is society's entrance fee (waived for children, the aged and infirm and some others). Without it, life could not go on: life in *any* kind of society. It is surely clear that this is not itself *sufficient* to give point to life: it is necessary if life is to have any point. Even the view that God meant man to work has to be explained: God meant man to be punished by work for his sin: and presumably the punishment is just and it is for the sake of paying the just penalty that man must work. Work may well be a necessary good rather than a necessary evil: but it is not itself a sufficient account of the meaning of life. If work means what one chooses to do, this may be very closely related to what gives life its meaning; we have to ask what the work is *for*. Here it might seem that a special case can be made for works of art. Some philosophers have claimed that these are done to promote some end: others that they are done for their own sake. It is the second view that interests us here. And all I have to say here is that I should not myself accept art as *the* thing that gives meaning to life: and for the same reason that I have rejected knowledge and the theoretic life (Chapter 3). We have to take other things into consideration. Clearly life may have a meaning even if one has work without meaning: certainly it may have a meaning for those whose work has come to nothing.

Is it possible to answer the question: Why am I here? by reference to an institution? I am here to serve my country, my church, my university, my class. How could it be that the institution is seen to have such authority? What could make it proper and even welcome to a man to die for his country?

Loyalty to country or church arises from something that just exists. Why should I be loyal to England and not to some country with a better record? The answer is simply that in fact I am English. We do not have a reason for being English: and surely in asking why am I a Christian, we may come sooner or later to a fact: I was born into Christendom. It is there and I belong to it. It had my first allegiance and if I am converted I am false to my first allegiance and can never be quite the same as the native adherents of the creed I join.

Loyalties arise out of the past. We have a rational enquiring interest in the past: what sort of causes lead us to what kinds of consequences? But the past interests historians (as it interests us all) not simply as a field of enquiry or a field in which certain laws are exemplified. The past interests us because it is 'our' past: we exist because it existed. Have I any *reason* for being interested in my own ancestors? Yes. Is it reasonable to attach particular importance to one's own ancestors or one's own past? It is not scientific, not narrowly rational: but in a broad sense it is reasonable to do so. Because this does count as a reason.

Loyalty to an institution arises from the fact that it exists and has existed through past years or ages. In a sense it would matter to its members, whatever kind of institution it was: and those who for good or bad reason oppose their own country or their own church, have to do violence to themselves. And it is important that these two great institutions claim our loyalty whatever their character may be. Of course we are inclined to break with our country if it seems to us to follow disgraceful ends or practise vicious means. But it is typical that this often feels like a temptation to treachery. And the situation is complicated by the fact that neither church nor state can be said to exist simply to achieve certain ends. What ends? Many of the things done by the state have to be done *because* it exists. The state does not exist because men want these things done: they want these things done because the state exists. And in fact this is commonly true of the church also. In either case it is possible after the event to provide an explanation to the effect that 'the state has a duty to provide a minimum subsistence for all its members'. But it was not designed to do this: it existed long before any such design was formed. The power of the state, because it *is there*, can be used for all sorts of purposes: but this is because the state has no definitive functions, no limit, no set of aims. Loyalty to the state may be rivalled and abraded by devotion to reasonable ideals: it may be enriched and strengthened by devotion to such ideals: it does not spring simply from any such devotion. Other institutions are fashioned to perform functions and men's attachment to them rests upon their devotion to the aims they serve. Men choose to join or leave them. But even here, as everybody knows, there is a tendency to be loyal just because they are there.[1]

Loyalty to an institution is to some people a first consideration: disloyalty the great sin (treason, treachery). To other people these notions mean very little. Can an institution stand up as an absolute in the world?

Institutions are the product of history and in the last analysis they are casualties of history. To claim an absolute position for an institution is a metaphysical claim. And metaphysical doctrines make such claims: the supremacy of society as the highest kind of individual, and of the state as the expression of the general will. These claims are made not for the purposes the state may serve: but for *the state itself* as an institution—designatable perhaps only by its actual sovereignty. But in fact states founder or fade out.

We can understand our world only by reference to its history: which means very largely the history of institutions. But it is hard to see why we must be bound by it. We are sometimes prompted by disloyalty, rejection, alienation; sometimes by loyalty. Even a sovereign institution which cannot be said to exist for this and that purpose, may in the end be rejected as serving no purpose or only a predominantly bad purpose. That it is *my country not another* I should be loyal to, may be an unarguable axiom: but it is not decisive. The given in-

[1] I derive these ideas about the state from Mr Rush Rhees.

stitution cannot be denied: but it can be criticised and opposed and abandoned.

In asking whether life has a meaning, we must take into account the actual existence of the state and other institutions. What I am now examining is the view that the state or the church can in itself give meaning to life.

I should say: it makes sense as an answer, because it is possible to claim an absolute existence for the state. The claim for the Church (which could be the institution embodying any historical religion) is bound up with claims about God and man. In the case of the purely ethical religions, the claim for the institution rests upon a condition: it is that it serves some ideal purpose—is functional. But in the case of the historical religions the institution is not merely functional. It is itself God's creation and that there is a Church is part of the Faith. The three great religions of the West have all included much Greek speculation: but they all also rest upon historical fact—'accident' as the outsider would call it. The Fourth Gospel, for example, begins with a discourse that could in itself be given a purely speculative or theoretical interpretation. Even 'the word was made flesh' has been so interpreted. But then it goes on: 'There was a man sent from God whose name was John.' And this man *called John* is the forerunner of the Christian Church. The historical religion, then, introduces the notion of an actual institution which has authority in itself and which claims either to be (in certain respects) immune from rational criticism, or itself to have the last word in any discussion about itself.

If these answers make sense, are they acceptable? There will always be two main lines of criticism of any such claims. First, that an actually existing authority, temporal or spiritual, may do the wrong things or do the right things in the wrong way. This criticism comes from the lovers of rational argument or of moral principle. Second, that loyalty to institutions may lead us to sacrifice ourselves and other people when we ought not to do so and especially to corrupt individuals into hypocrisy. Are we to say that man was made for the state or the church? The truth seems to be that in the case of these sovereign institutions this proposition and its converse are both over-simplifications. Criticisms of the first kind can be doctrinaire; of the second kind, sentimental. But criticisms of either kind can be valid. If so, the *absolute* claim on behalf of an institution is never valid. Institutions contribute enormously to the meaning of life; they are perhaps necessary conditions for it to have a meaning. But not in themselves sufficient.

What may I live for? What may I live by? One answer that can honestly be given by many people in our own society is: My family. In a sense there is an institution of family life: with different forms in different classes and cultures. But of course the family itself is a natural fact, characteristic of mammalian life in general. It is the focus for two fundamental instincts: in the system of means and ends in nature, it can hardly be denied that mating and reproducing are the principal point of life. The family as a group is universal in the sense that everyone has two parents, and the usual cohorts of ancestors. And those who are in the phase of getting married and having children often have a strong desire to show that they are just like everybody else—however implausible this may appear to the onlooker. It is, I believe, quite a common feeling that one is being used up in parenthood —played with, knocked about, worn out—*and that this does not matter*. Men and women who have deeply resented any idea of being anyone else's property, do not object to being their children's property: most astonishing of all they do not object to losing their youth. I think this feeling is not peculiar to the idealistic or romantic or reflective parent. And at bottom it is a feeling that there is point to what one does and endures. On the other hand not having children is recognised in all societies as a great natural evil, comparable with infirmity and death and loss of liberty. To lose children by death is commonly regarded as the greatest of all bereavements: as something in a sense contrary to nature, however common an occurrence it may still be.

Can we accept the purely biological determination of the meaning of our life? Animals do not accept a meaning of life: in a sense they act as if they did. But even in their case, to continue the species by mating and reproduction is the principal but not the only end of life. Even amongst the higher animals, to go on living, eating, sleeping, playing, fighting, is an aim even for those who are excluded from having offspring. In some cases their continued existence serves the reproductive end indirectly—by providing a circle of uncles and aunts who can at least provide food and warmth and keep off enemies. If animals can be said to enjoy life, then clearly they enjoy it in many ways which are of no evolutionary significance. Even in the most doctrinaire biological terms it does not make sense to say simply that what animals are here for is to reproduce their kind. Unless there is some point in there being rabbits why should there be any point in mating and producing rabbits? And if there is a point in there being rabbits, this means creatures with variety in their lives—not only mating but also fighting and washing their faces. Even the activities which are obviously of use to the species (like the belligerence of cocks and bulls, the territorial defences of robins) can be thought of as what it means to be a member of the species, as well as a device for continuing the species.

This is (at the very least) how we should have to consider the human family: a complex of behaviour and feeling which is both biologically useful and characteristically human. If we look for the meaning of life here, it cannot lie simply in the continuation of the race. Nor the continuation of a given line. Unless there is some point in being one of the Joneses there cannot be any point in producing an heir to all the Joneses. A person cannot surely see the *whole* point of life in having a child; or if he does, he must support that view on non-biological grounds (for example, the point of having children is to add to the number of immortal souls and to have a chance of adding to the number of the elect).

Strong as this feeling for the family is, it must include the notion that there is point not only in there being a new generation, but in the life of each individual. Without the family the individual may be spiritually diminished: this consideration is based not on the fact that without the family there would be no individuals, but on the character of the individual himself.

The family then enjoys this natural basis—making it an end open to people in general without reference to special talents or skills. And there are clearly many forces at work in society which add to the appeal of the family.

Children need their parents and especially their mothers. Many women soon find that their own children are the only people who have ever uniquely needed them. This gives a point and purpose in life so long as the need lasts: and the need can clearly be prolonged by upbringing. The need becomes reversed: it is the parents who need their children. But the situation can be equal and satisfying on both sides.

Parents enjoy a second childhood in the infancy of their own family. They have had to do without childish things for many years: and many childish pleasures may have been altogether forbidden to them by their own parents. In a family, the father and the mother have an opportunity to enjoy these things vicariously—watching their children, turning a blind eye when they learn they are doing the things they were not allowed to do. This may build up a tremendous interest in one's own children and sometimes in children in general—or children of the age one is inclined to identify oneself with. And of course there is also the very general consideration that children are *promising:* and their promise contrasts with the parents' own performance. Romantic literature is built very largely on the themes of childhood and youth, clearly setting 'the budding rose above the rose full blown'.

This can give rise to the view that the life of the child is central and lends value to the life of his parents: that the family is important not because it finally produces a new generation of adults, but because it is the essential condition for the *life of children*.

It was against this sort of view that D. H. Lawrence grumbled to a correspondent: He did not want to hear about their children: people *ought to be* much more interesting than their children. Certainly the view can rest upon a kind of fallacy. The view of children which only a grown-up can have, is a part of the life of a grown-up and not of a child. It is something (commonly) to be thankful for—like the sight of a running stag or a basking seal. 'That there is pleasure there' is often true: but the reflective view of the experienced (and perhaps distorted) mind is not part of the life of the child or the stag or the seal. They have a life but they do not see it as we see it. We might say our view is a fantasy or vision inspired by them. And in fact it can be a vitally important factor in the life of an adult. Family life provides essential conditions of life for children: it may also provide a light and glow in the life of the parents. There may be a certain element of exploitation—whether by parents of their children, or by children of their parents. But a fair balance can be achieved even including some such elements.

There are then two views about the family. That it is the place for people to live the most human life: that it is the place for children to lead child-like lives. That the real point of the family rests entirely on the second consideration seems to me not to bear examination. But children are people: and not all children become adults. We can say then that the value of the family consists in its being the place for children and the way for children to grow up: and the way for parents to enjoy their own adult view of childhood and to exercise their own adult view of parenthood.

How far does this go in showing that family life provides the point of our existence? Some people seem to find it sufficient. In present-day society there is great emphasis on the family as the source of morality, the proper focus for religion and the unit of economic spending-power. Churches, both Protestant and Catholic, take the family as a kind of model: the Church is the family of God, which means the family of the church-going families. Much that is said about 'the family' seems to apply to the group of the father-mother-dependent children and to do nothing for single men and women and childless couples, except to emphasise their loneliness and unenviable atypicality. (The Gospel view of the human family is of course quite another thing.) The state supports it or pretends to support it: about three-quarters of all advertising (outside the main fields of alcohol, tobacco and cosmetics) is aimed at 'family spending'. And when the family is not being flattered and used it is being blamed—what else can we blame for the failings of children? And at the most serious level, research into emotional disturbances and mental disorder is forever finding the cause in the pattern of family relationships especially as these affect the child early in life. The family *is* fundamental as well as useful.[1]

But 'life' is not synonymous with 'family life'. The child grows up and cuts loose and there may be long years during which the whole idea of family life is a matter of duty and embarrassment. And in every generation a surprising number of men and of women remain unmarried. This used to be thought a matter of choice for men and necessity for women: but now it is clear that it may be choice or necessity for either sex. At all events many people are obliged to go through one of the most difficult periods of life—first jobs, first failures—outside the family: and the business of finding a marriage partner is commonly also completed without family help. For those who marry it seems clear that the new home and children matter far more today than at any past time. The enormous reduction of 'working hours' has led to more and more home-duties by both parents. But these parents may still be quite young when their children leave home. For some this leaves a tremendous gap in their lives which nothing can ever fill again. But others, in time, will admit that they are glad for what they have had but glad that their family days are over.

Miss Ivy Compton-Burnett, in a broadcast talk, denied that she had ever said that the family was totally bad. 'No,' she said, 'there is always the link between the siblings.' This can last through a long life: it certainly remains important (for those who have siblings) in most

[1] See D. W. Winnicott: *The Child and the Family*, 1957.

ranks of society in spite of separation in place and status. But here, as a rule, we are talking of only one amongst very many ties: for if a man must leave his father and mother in order to take a wife, still more must he turn from his sisters and brothers.

Butler said that every one of our passions and affections has its natural stint and bound: and if this be exceeded the result is never profitable and often is 'downright pain and misery'. This would seem to be as true of family affections as of other necessary passions. And though it is necessary in general, it is not in fact available for all. Those who enjoy a good family relationship are certainly less inclined to ask whether life has any meaning. It does not follow that they have in fact found it.

What we are here for is to serve others; to do what good we can; to leave the world a better place than we found it—or, less optimistically, to leave the world not as badly off as it would have been if we had never been born.

This is available to all: does not depend upon the existence of particular relationships. It is or seems less narrow than the family: and in fact family considerations often have to be sacrificed to the wider view. It is an explicit view, often heard and deeply-held, which in fact gives direction to many lives. But again it is often very generally and vaguely expressed: since finally we cannot attempt to do all the good we see needs doing, we have to look for scope and opportunity to pursue some particular good for our fellow men. And here it can well be that one is left with no opportunity or nothing to base a decision on. To do good certainly will involve us sooner or later in a further decision: *What* good?

That this is the point and purpose of life is often argued or explained on theological grounds. There are two great commandments: Thou shalt love the Lord thy God, and Thou shalt love thy neighbour as thyself. The second is often interpreted as living one's life for others. The two are connected. We serve men because God commands it: because in helping, rescuing, visiting those who need it we are directly serving God. The main Christian tradition (both Protestant and Catholic) is that we have an additional sacramental duty to God: but some have always been compelled to think that to love God is to love my neighbour. Abou Ben Adhem was convinced of this in his dream.[1]

The very important point about these theological views is that my living for others is not thought to justify itself. My fellow men are not necessarily any more worth-while than I am myself: and viewed dispassionately we might well decide that to devote one's life to the service of one's fellow men is to waste it on an unworthy object. What is there about them that obliges me to find the point and purpose of my life in serving them? The theological views answer that what we are to do is to serve God (and there cannot be any question about the value of this): and that

[1] In Leigh Hunt's sonnet, Abou Ben Adhem (while dreaming) saw an angel writing down in a book the names of those that love God. He told the angel to put down his name as one who loves his fellow men. In a further dream he saw the angel again, and the book: 'And lo! Ben Adhem's name led all the rest.'

we are to do so by serving others—and Christ died for even the least and the lowest of them. These are effective arguments, not sentimental about ourselves or others. But of course they imply that ultimately the point of my life is to do as God commands.

The view that I am here to serve others is characteristic of much humanistic and ostensibly non-religious think-ing. Something like it was to be (in J. S. Mill's opinion) the ideal of men in the future—a non-theistic religion. But how is this view to be justified? If the theological arguments are rejected, is there any reason for saying that the meaning of my life is to serve my fellow men? Since 'my' refers to any speaker, presumably those whom I serve may find the point of their lives in serving me and others. Or they may not.

I want to distinguish this view of the meaning of life from the much more restricted proposition that I have a *duty* to do good to others.[1] We have lots of duties and many of them to certain people. I owe a duty to a creditor, to a benefactor, a dependant, an employer, to anyone I happen to have made a promise to. I can be said to have a duty to anyone I am addressing—not to deceive him by what I say. But beyond all these duties to assignable

[1] When Kant said that we are designed by Nature not for serving our own happiness but for doing our duty, he certainly did not mean by 'doing our duty', doing our duty *to other people*. Many duties are not *to* other people (in his view): perhaps strictly speaking, duties are duties, and not *to anybody*. I suspect that those who say 'we are here to do our duty' have in mind serving other people or perhaps institu-tions (my station and its duties). The mere dedication to duty as such (no particular content supposed) does not in fact seem to be the popular view: Kant thought it was.

persons, it is commonly held that I have a duty to do good to those who are in need. But this cannot mean that I have a duty to everyone in need: it must be a matter which depends on occasion, opportunity and resources—and, of course, on other obligations. I have a duty to give only as I am reasonably able to give. The Good Samaritan fulfilled this duty: the Priest and the Levite failed to do their duty. What indicated the duty was of course coming upon a very obvious and urgent need. This apparent and overwhelming need picked itself out from all other possible objects of benevolence. And clearly a principle of selection is necessary: we cannot satisfy all the needs we meet and of course we could discover endless further needs if we set about the task in earnest.

To say this is a duty is a very different thing from saying that it is the point and justification of my life. (Nobody is likely to say that the point of life is to pay debts or taxes.) Can it be argued or has it to be taken (or left) on its own merits?

Like the notion of the duty of benevolence, the ideal of serving our fellow men has to become selective. It will often amount to the view that what makes life worth while is showing compassion, understanding and forgiveness; giving help as one can and especially giving help to those who ask it: and perhaps also devoting time and effort to some enterprise which will relieve suffering or increase happiness in others.

What I now offer is a critique of this non-theological view of life.

(1) It is not so evident that it is available to everybody.

Kant may be quite correct in saying that we can all fulfill our *duty* of beneficence whatever our inclinations or characters may be. But this is something more: we are thinking of beneficence as what makes sense of my life. Many people are so made that entering fully and readily and acceptably into the lives of others is difficult for them: it seems to go *against their nature*. If they find they have a duty to do so, they may do it at immense cost to themselves—and knowing that their effort cannot really be wholly acceptable to the beneficiary. Kant says that a person who does this is not the meanest of God's creatures and this is evidently a just judgement. But for such a person, a life of self-devotion to others cannot seem to make sense of his own life.

(2) Why is it so important to serve *others*: why is this somehow on a different plane from serving myself? In my view this shows an incoherence, a lack of reflexion, a sentimental bias, a weakness, a concealment. Of course there is a difference between helping others and helping myself: the first is commonly a social act, involving the intercourse of minds, a life together, a mutual relationship, altogether lacking in simply helping myself. But in helping someone else am I not to suppose that he will also want to help others—and sometimes to help me? And if I should not help A at B's expense, why should I help A at my expense? The answer is of course that in the second case I waive my rights, I am consenting to my own act and my own forfeit. If B consented, then I could help A at B's expense. But I cannot believe that it is consistent with my regarding myself as a rational being and a member of

society, that I should have no regard to my own rights. Moreover there is something wrong (in such a stance) in my view of others. Why should they acquiesce in my treating myself simply as a means of benefiting them? Living for others is no good unless it means first of all living with others. *Altruism* is not able to stand up to scrutiny.

(3) 'Because we are in a peculiar manner, as I may speak, intrusted with ourselves: and therefore care of our own interests, as well as of our conduct, particularly belongs to us.'[1] This says something of the importance of being able to stand upright unaided. And surely it is important: and something of a limitation upon the doctrine of living for others as it is often presented. Even the religious notion of charity is often misinterpreted in a manner which leads people to undermine the solidity of those they benefit or try to benefit. I am certainly not trying to belittle the virtue: but it more often means understanding and less often means taking charge, than traditional teaching suggests. Again I am certainly not proposing self-sufficiency as an ideal in itself. This comment is really a gloss on the preceding one. It is in mutual and often unplanned, unregulated relationships that the great bonus lies. And these are not possible on a doctrine of simple self-denial.[2]

(4) However, not everyone finds it possible to build up mutual relationships. A mutual relationship does not mean one in which A's relation to B and B's relation to A are of

[1] Butler: *Sermons*, XII.
[2] See also Chapter 8, pp. 184–5.

the same character. In the case of parent and child this cannot properly be so. What makes a relationship mutual is something that satisfies both parties. For some, an asymmetrical relationship can do something to satisfy and to give a point to life. One of the great weaknesses of all these popular informal answers, is that they seem to think that the same answer will do for everybody. But this is evidently not the case.

A fourth answer: What I am here for is to realise to the full whatever is my own nature: to be myself as fully as I can. The aim is being rather than doing: and this view is that the point of my life cannot be found in other people but must be found in me. People must count in themselves and not just because of what they can be for others. But people differ in what they are and what they may be. They must be allowed to develop in their own way: restraint is in itself bad. But so also is idleness, frivolity, timidity.

So the argument would proceed from making a kind of logical point against 'living for others', to a broad humanistic view. We are here with talents, opportunities, choices, encounters: as rational beings we must wish to live fully, to *be* something. What is *given* is not a status, a task, nor even a fixed character: what is given is an opportunity *to be*. Why am I here? The answer is: To be myself.

This view certainly need not be selfish or self-centred: it is in a sense serious—to ask the question is itself serious: but it need not be solemn or pretentious. It is likely to be

strenuous but one can come to recognise (as Wordsworth
and Mill did) that our passive sensibilities are even more
important than our active powers.

This is still highly general. We most of us feel that we
might have been somebody very different and in fact we
often feel we might still become somebody very different.
We have to ask: Which of my possible selves am I to
become? This often looks like a very open question. And
there is always the possibility that, surveying the different
selves I might become, I *dislike them all*. Unless we have
some principle to guide our choice, then the answer, To
be yourself, still does not tell me what I am here for.

But is there a choice? Many people doubt whether there
is. Then what I am here for is to be what I cannot in any
case avoid being. Of course such a view allows development: I am to become something but there is no choice
as to what I am to become. If this view is supposed to
inspire me, to offer me some practical guidance, it comes
into question: Is this logically coherent? The difficulty is
like that which haunts Dialectical Materialism. Necessary
social laws govern man's progress: but he is nevertheless
exhorted to play an active voluntary part in history. To
reject the Marxist aim is to be rejected by history. However we *can* do it. And if I were to believe that my own
story will work itself out in accordance with necessary
laws—nevertheless, I could decline to accept this fate as
the meaning of my life. I *could* decide it had no meaning.

In reaction against such deterministic views, some
people see the meaning of life in freedom itself. To make
a choice may seem to limit me, to define me, and so to

determine what I must become. But this (it is said) is not really the case. We can always undo our choices, escape from our characters. What do we escape into? The dignity and the burden of human life lies in making choices. 'Self-realisation' would be to enslave oneself in an idea, a notion, an essence;—or it would be to pretend to be so enslaved. To *be* is not to be this or that *kind* of person (as a thing is this or that kind of thing without the possibility of escape). To be is to be free.

That the end and meaning of life is to be myself is (I think) true by definition. It does not limit me. It says at least something about what it is to be a person: that it is for that person to say for himself whether this or that gives life a meaning. Choice is *my* choice. I cannot simply be told by someone else—although of course I may be enlightened or convinced by somebody else. But while to choose belongs to a rational being, it implies choosing with reason, choosing one thing and rejecting another. Choices might be compared with promises: one does not make them for their own sake but for a reason. However the mere ideal of self-realisation does not itself provide a reason.

Here again we find we are considering necessary conditions for life to have a meaning: not a sufficient account of what the meaning is.

In discussing the question: What is the highest of all goods achievable by man? Aristotle says that the many sometimes think it is pleasure. This is represented as an almost totally unreflective view. These people are inarticulate, but to judge from the way they live, one would say they took pleasure to be the goal and end of life. No doubt Aristotle here has in mind those whose only idea of pleasure is bodily pleasure, especially lust. Later on when he has given his own much wider meaning to pleasure (including very much what we mean by enjoyments), Aristotle says that the many always connect the notion of a happy life (or a good kind of life) with pleasure. And he says they are quite correct in doing so: and it would be absurd to suppose that a good life was not a pleasant or enjoyable one.

Can it be seriously held that what I am here for is to enjoy life, to find pleasure in living? Not, I believe, if we think of the pleasures as a restricted range of sensations or experiences. Perhaps this is indeed what many people live for: but would any reflective person say that they had found 'the meaning of life': are they not missing the meaning? And are they at all interested in whether it has a meaning or not?

However, here again, I think there is a valid point: something which is a necessary condition for there to be a meaning in life. To do things for pleasure often means to do them for their own sake.[1] If people are asked why they dance or sing or ride or swim or read novels or make love, they may say: for the pleasure of it. And this implies that they are speaking of things they do for their own sake— not (or not simply) for some further end. And here Aristotle is surely absolutely right. If life is to have a meaning at all, there must be things we do and enjoy for

[1] Hume: *Enquiry concerning Morals*, Appendix I, v.

themselves. This again is a logical and a decisive argument. And it does at least constitute a refutation of some popular forms of hedonism. If we sing or eat or make love or read books for their own sake, then we do not do them for the sake of *something else* called 'pleasure'.

However it does not tell us what things are enjoyable on their own account: what things are worth while in themselves. Here again we are left with a choice. In Chapter 8 I shall try to consider further what are the necessary and sufficient conditions for answering the second question.

CHAPTER 5

THE FIRST QUESTION

LET US SUPPOSE that the first question is taken to have a purely theoretical meaning: that is to say it asks for some account of how the world as we know it came into existence. This also gives a purely theoretical sense to the second question: for granted that we can say how the world came into existence it must surely be the world as a going concern, working partly at least according to laws: for many of these we already think we know. Explain how the world as we know it came into existence as a going concern at least partly systematic, and the system will offer some sort of theoretical explanation (no doubt very incomplete) of how the various species of animals came into existence: and so how particular specimens came into existence. And I am a particular specimen of a particular species of animal.

Of course, the living things on this planet do not occupy a central position in the world as we know it, so long as our point of view is strictly theoretical. I have spoken of the world as we know it and I mean the universe of matter as we are coming to know it. This is very big: some theories support the view that it cannot be all that much bigger than it at present appears at Mount Palomar: but this is by no means decided. At all events we begin with a universe in space composed of what we might as well call matter: the elements of which have many of them been identified: and existing in various physical conditions of density, temperature, integration, many of them familiar enough from observation of the earth. It is a natural supposition that these different states are successive: so that we can say that some of the masses are more developed than others and this provides us with a basis for constructing in outline the stages through which each has passed or is passing. To discover which are in the 'earliest' identifiable stage is, of course, a problem of immense interest: and a puzzle arises as to why some masses are at a more advanced stage than others. So the question 'Why is there anything at all?' is in effect replaced by the question: 'What is the "earliest" identifiable stage of matter from which we may suppose that the "later" stages developed and how did this process come about?' So also the question: 'Why is there just what there is and not something different?' takes on a new look. We could for a moment take it to mean Why are things of a certain temperature and not much hotter or colder? and, of course, this has to be broken up into the question Why have some things now a certain temperature and are they getting hotter or colder and, if so, according to what general law? Or we might for the moment take the question to mean: Why are there the elements there are and not others? Here again the answer might be first of all that there may be others: and secondly, if it appears that some elements developed out of others, we ask which are the oldest and most fundamental ones at the preceding epoch. And so we go back to the "oldest' *kinds* of thing there are that we have yet identified.

In short, the tremendous question about the origin of all that is gives way to an immense number of questions about the origin of particular elements or particular states. And, of course, the way to tackle these is highly sophisticated: and although it is experimentally controlled it is still speculative.

Perhaps this is the chief importance here of size or scale. It is absolutely useless to approach these problems with terrestrial notions of size, above all with our common everyday notions of apparent size. We all know (although we so often forget) that size, distance, age, speed, are all relative notions: and that it is in a sense a mistake even to be unduly impressed by such expressions as: 'a billion light-years'. That is to say it is a mistake for anyone whose interests are strictly theoretical. So that when Pascal admitted that these vast spaces terrified him he was not writing in the scientific idiom. Why should not one galaxy be a million light-years away from another? In its own context, the distance is suitable enough. Does it matter that it makes us feel very small? David Hume, in similar vein, asks why we should worry about the smallness of a mite.

'This, however, is certain, that we can form ideas which shall be no greater than the smallest atom of the animal spirits of an insect a thousand times less than a mite.'[1]

Does that make us so very *big*? This also is irrelevant.

[1] *Treatise of Human Nature*, Book i, Part ii, §1.

But for the scientist who is interested in cosmology and cosmogony, size certainly matters very much indeed. This is because so much is speculative in his views: that is to say, so much depends on calculations and deductions from relatively few measured distances or sizes: and errors in calculation or measurement can result in absolutely tremendous differences. If these theories were aimed at securing practical results, this would be virtually self-defeating. All the scientist aims at is some sort of theory that will be worth further serious examination.

Could such enquiries have practical results? Yes: in two ways. What we can learn about the material universe may have application to terrestrial processes. (The converse has most certainly proved itself.) Conceivably we might discover new sources of energy, new ways of working the materials of the world for our own purposes. We may learn to reach other planets, other solar systems: I mean some people may some day find they can, if they want to or need to, go and live there. And I have no doubt that when this happens the effects on human life and thought and manners will be tremendous. But the scientist enquiring into the nature of the material universe will regard this as a secondary matter. (If *he* decided to go, it would be for the same sort of reason that leads scientists nowadays to emigrate: the conditions of research would be more favourable.) These practical consequences are a feature of all 'pure' science and have no particular connexion with any practical interpretation of the two questions.

But, of course, there is a second possible practical result —in learning about the stages of different systems of matter we speculate into the future as well as into the past. We might in this way come to accept the view that certain of the more familiar systems (and this will mean the smaller ones) are on their way out. Perhaps we can estimate their life as a surveyor might estimate the life of a house. As we all know, this has been done for one of the planets: the one we all (so far) occupy. The estimate seems to us an ample one: if any of us think of it at all, we have to consider what it would be like for people (very likely some of them our descendants or very distant cousins) to contemplate the finish.

This might have some bearing on the practical version of the original question: the meaning of it all. We ask not only why it is here in the sense of where did it come from. We also ask where it is going—or 'what is it all in aid of?' And just as the question about the origin of all things, when seriously tackled in a theoretical spirit, gives way to highly technical questions about how this may have developed out of that: so the question about the end towards which it all leads, gives place to particular questions about the development and ultimate extinction of this or that particular system. We have certainly a practical (if very remote) interest in the end of this earth and its accessible neighbours. But we also have a practical (and very, very remote) interest in its origin and the origin of the material system from which it emerged. We must notice that neither of these is of particular interest to the purely theoretical enquirer. But is this practical interest exactly what we have in mind when we ask about 'the meaning of it all'? If I own a house I have a practical interest in the way it was made, how old it is, what external hazards of weather, earthquake, it has to stand up to: how long it will last: how readily I could then move to another. These are indeed interests of mine even if I ignore them—have no concern about them, do not *take* any interest in them. It may be that I do investigate these questions and decide I have in fact nothing to bother me. Or I may forget all about them and be lucky or unlucky. The theories of cosmologists certainly have this practical interest and it may or may not give rise to a practical concern. And if it does, is it to be identified with the particular concern expressed in our questions?

The practical interest in cosmology is essentially forward-looking. If I ask how and of what materials my house *was* made, my concern is for the length of life I can expect it to have: and whether there is anything I could now do to strengthen it. Or even where I could go if it fell down. This seems to me just the kind of practical interest which scientists' theories about the earth and its neighbours have for all of us. And the striking thing is that this practical interest is pretty remote and unlikely to cause us that painful or anxious concern we have over phenomena of smaller scale: nuclear fission, overpopulation, new diseases. Again it is not peculiar to the theoretical enquiry about the nature of the universe as such and apart from human action.

So that my conclusions so far would be that cosmology does not answer directly the main question: Where did it all come from: and the answers it gives to the question: Where is it all going to, what is it all in aid of? turn out to be so reassuring that it becomes more, not less, surprising that this question should be taken very seriously, as it undoubtedly is.

However, there is, of course, something to add. The *way* in which these questions are dealt with by scientists, rather than the particular answers they give to particular questions, is what is relevant to the main questions. They treat of particular systems of matter: the origin of these systems and their prospects. And they take it for granted that once a non-elementary system develops it goes through stages and hazards and finally disintegrates. The systems which are so far regarded as elementary might in a sense be said to be those which have as yet had no history known to us, e.g. hydrogen atoms in vast groups. This amounts to saying that everything we know comes from (say) hydrogen atoms: and we know (as yet) nothing about what *they* came from.

Would a scientist ever say more: That hydrogen atoms are the *first* cause of all the world as we know it? Would he have to say that they had always been there? I am inclined to think he would say: 'Always is not for me: I take things step by step, piecemeal—however long the steps and however large the pieces.'

What the scientist offers as 'a reason for all that exists' is the distribution and the uniformities of change that he discovers within the existents he can reach. If beyond all he has so far posited he saw good reason to believe in some still more remote existent from which the hitherto known world developed, this would of course be thought of in very much the same way as the material world and of course it would be thought of as something in the universe, not outside it. The reason for all that is can for the scientist mean no more than the order discoverable within changing systems of matter.

It seems to me that this does not tell us what we want to know when we ask what is the meaning of it all: why does anything exist and why just what there is and not something else: what is it all *for*? Of course if anybody feels that the scientific questions *are* what he had in mind in asking about the meaning of it all, that is well enough: let him pursue his satisfaction there. But if anybody wants to answer these questions in a different sense, he should notice that science does not ask them: that it tries to discover orders of different kinds within the material world and that it treats of no ultimate beginning or end. However, it does treat of the beginnings of systems and of their ends.

If this is the utmost that science could tell us about the origin of the world as we know it, why has the 'First Cause' so long been treated with very great respect by most religions, by the arts and by most philosophers? Why 'First Cause'? Strictly this ought to mean original antecedent cause (what is called the 'efficient cause'): that thing or event which started everything off: an explosion perhaps, or a collision. But in trying to explain what there is, scientists cannot confine themselves strictly to efficient causes. We want to know not merely what started something off, but how it did so, the law according to which its consequences followed. The nature of things and their distribution are both needed in the explanation: and this nature of things (or 'formal cause') is an essential concept of science. The two are complementary. We may think of the fall of an acorn as the efficient cause of the oak tree that grows from it: but only because we know something about the nature, form, pattern, order of events proper to acorns. Without such law-like knowledge we certainly could not say that the acorn was the efficient cause. Conversely we could not know that an oak tree will (or may) grow up *just here* unless we know an acorn has fallen here.

The First Cause can be understood as both formal and efficient, but neither of these entitles it to anything more than the greatest theoretical interest. What gave it its numinous character was undoubtedly the supposition that the First Cause must have somehow had in mind a plan of the world that was to follow from it: and this implies that it must have been an intelligence. The First Cause was thought of as Final Cause, too: as having *an end in view* from the very beginning: an intelligence such as was obliged to work out things the way it did. For what was there to oblige or coerce the First Cause? What was planned and executed (or initiated) was also chosen: the agency cannot have been external. But if internal, then it must have had that power to act which intelligences sometimes enjoy: that is, the power of the will. So from the earliest days of philosophy honest and rigorous thinkers have spoken of the First Cause with reverence and awe. I am thinking of philosophers not in holy orders: not of priests or prophets or shamans. Of course they have not always agreed: some have emphasised will rather than intelligence: others—on the whole with very much happier consequences for mankind—have emphasised intelligence. And in characteristic Greek–Christian fashion, they have often included moral attributes as being a proper part of intelligence. (How can the intelligence fail to know good and evil: and if so, how fail to love the good and hate the evil?)

David Hume, who never tired himself (although he sometimes tired his readers) in deriding the concepts of popular religion, admits that the concept of First Cause as intelligence and will, is a philosophical concept: it makes sense. He himself prefers to think of First Cause as simply efficient-formal cause: whether what we call dead matter or something like what we call vegetable matter. But the other notions are not dismissed as 'sick man's fancies' nor as 'getting us into fairyland'. Hume argues from the evidence about intelligence and will and the moral attributes: he thinks the evidence is against them. (Hume cannot be tied down to one kind of argument: he sometimes says that even First Cause itself is an empty notion in this context: and he also says that the moral attributes make *no sense* when applied to it.)

Was Hume in error in taking *this* sense of First Cause as a general philosophical concept? Is he confusing the notion of a primitive cause (or group of causes) within the world as we know it, with the notion of a cause external to the world, the cause of the universe? I think he sometimes means the one and sometimes the other: and that he produces valid objections to the accepted concept of 'the cause of the universe': objections which Kant argued more clearly. In arguing *for* conceivable First Causes (e.g. something somewhat like vegetable matter) he is surely thinking of a primitive cause *within* nature. In arguing *against* theological views he often seems to be treating of the cause *of* the universe. In arguing from the evidence that if God created the universe he must be deficient in intelligence or moral goodness or power, he uses theological concepts. The view that really emerges in his moral works would make this whole discussion about God's moral character meaningless: and while this view is compatible with taking the First Cause as a primordial cause or set of causes within nature, it is I think doubtful whether the First Cause should be described as intelligence or will. Can intelligence and will really be denied a moral character?

Hume's positive contribution to the subject is to show that 'philosophers' or scientists will look only for causes within nature and will want some sort of evidence for supposing they are really *there*: and they will not even raise the question of their moral character.[1] Suppose all animal life, as well as all the host of elements, developed by the working of some laws from a vegetable substance or from groups of hydrogen atoms. Who will ask about

[1] See Hume's *Dialogues concerning Natural Religion* (cf. Philo in Part II, p. 185, and Part VII, p. 219), and *Enquiry concerning Human Understanding*, §11. On the moral attributes, *Dialogues*, Part II (Demea), and *Enquiry concerning Morals*, Appendix I (end).

their moral character? At least Hume cannot be mistaken in arguing that this might be the conclusion reached about the oldest causes known to have been (and to be) at work in nature. And Hume rightly says that inferred causes of this kind can have no practical importance in themselves. The consequences of these causes are the world we live in, including animals and people and their institutions. Of course these have practical importance. These speculative First Causes are known to us only by their observed effects. Their importance can lie only in these effects: i.e. in what we already knew to be important before we began our enquiry. It is the nature of the world we know that is of practical importance to us. And this is a magnificent truism. These observed effects (and the laws they now act by) are our world and we can survive only if we attach practical importance to them. (Otherwise, as Hume elsewhere remarks, 'human nature must immediately perish and go to ruin.'[1]) But where they came from does not matter: and how we ought to live our lives is not determined by the conditions of our survival. Many of the worst survive along with the best: many of the best die along with the worst.

But Hume is also prepared to admit that amongst these primordial causes, there *may* be an intelligence and a will. Is this totally mistaken? Ought he to have admitted this as a possibility? It seems to me that he was correct at that stage to discuss it as a possibility. For in a sense it is quite undeniable that in many of its workings, nature gives an appearance of design and contrivance. It seems that parts

[1] *Treatise of Human Nature*, Book I, Part iv, §4.

and movements are so arranged as to produce certain important effects. Living things were known to have a life cycle which could be accomplished only if all their parts and movements were adjusted with the greatest precision: and further research has shown how much more delicate the structure, how much more widespread the adjustment. Leibniz's vision of living things as gardens, every bloom of which is itself a garden *ad infinitum* is not so wide of the mark.[1] We have only to assume that the life cycle was the aim, to suppose that the adaptations which permit it were arranged by an artificer who had this aim in mind. And certainly we are familiar with the notion of planning to make and making according to plan: we do it every day. Hume of course accepts the notion of this kind of explanation. If we found a flint arrow or a plough-share or a book or an automobile or a computer we should infer that some intelligent being had planned and constructed it according to his plan. Are we to take the same view of oak trees or daffodils or mice or men? Of course we do not. We know by experience that books are made by men and that trees are not. Trees come from seed and seed from earlier trees. But in Hume's day it was supposed that a species of a living thing was changeless, permanent, from the very beginning. Hume himself refers to 'the eternal frame and constitution of animals'. The planning then is not of this oak tree but of the species: and the series was started off by the construction of one or more specimens which were so made as to go on (in favourable conditions) producing very many acorns and a suitable

[1] *Monadology*, § 67.

selection of trees. And of course it was required that the different species be considered together (the bees to carry the pollen etc.): and with them their sources of nourishment and even their destroyers. (It was not designed that the whole earth should be covered with oak trees.) Now we come down to soils, rocks, climates, atmospheres: and the planning of all was interdependent. Admittedly it was not so easy to isolate the inanimate kinds as the animate ones which seemed to be marked by their peculiar mode of propagation. Locke had already shown some doubt as to whether our knowledge of the metals and other lower orders would ever reach finality. But it was not at all necessary to suppose we could identify all the kinds or elements—merely that they were there and must have been planned.

Nowadays we try to explain that species are not eternal: that they die out because circumstances or their enemies overcome them: they leave no progeny and that is their end. But also we claim that new species evolve from others by the occurrence of new inherited characteristics which enable them to survive where others perish. The theory has many weaknesses but of course its standing is in no doubt. It purports to show that, given a long enough time, all possible varieties of living creatures will appear and those whose genetic characteristics are favourable in their environment survive: the others do not. They disappear 'from natural causes'. Hence the survivors appear well adapted to their neighbours and environment because they *are* well adapted.

Hume lacks the notion of a law (a natural law) of

adaptation. He in one place explicitly says that there is no evidence that any species has ever become extinct.[1] But although he has no particular explanation to offer, he suggests that the various species of living things could all have developed from vegetable matter: and perhaps this from inanimate matter. But in fact he has two main arguments against the existence of a designed world. First, that we cannot say of any organism: It must have had an intelligent designer. There is no 'must' about it. We know from experience that some things have intelligent designers and never occur except through plan and contrivance. We know this of books: we also know it of ploughshares. The first are tremendously complex but it is not because they are so complex that we see that they must have been constructed by intelligence. (Ploughshares are quite certainly the work of smiths but they are very simple objects indeed.) Books are not more complex than trees: but we know by experience that books do not grow from seed and trees do. Second: the one thing we can assert with confidence is that everything we recognise as contrived was made by man or animal and men and animals are not contrived. From artifacts we are at once led by experience back to natural objects—the artificers. There is no such powerful argument from natural objects back to artificers.

This is Hume's theory and it also is a scientific argument so far as it goes. Its weakness is that Hume in his day was unable to offer us any suggestion as to the origin and development of living things. Its strength is its refusal to

[1] *Dialogues concerning Natural Religion*, XI, Philo.

accept the theory put forward (contrivance or design) as the only possible theory: and its implicit insistence that if there were any such divine artificers we should have some better evidence of them.

But did any of the more rational theologians of Hume's day (represented in the *Dialogues* by 'Cleanthes') really expect to find this? Possibly not. I suppose they held that from the evidence of adaptation one could argue inevitably to contrivance. They often spoke as though the adaptation was all-embracing: just as determinists often argue as though universal causation implies that everything affects and is affected by everything else. But this is not so. We can say there are conjunctions in nature which are accidental: we can say that some creatures are better adapted to their environment than others: and that even a well-adapted species by no means implies a favourable adaptation of all its individual members. Granted that the adaptation is only partial, it of course remains tremendously *impressive*. And if it is held that it leads inevitably to the inference of design then one thinks of designers of immense intelligence, foresight and power. If the limitations of adaptation are not stressed, one thinks of a single designer of boundless intelligence, foresight and power: and it is a natural transition to add his good will towards the things he has made. What if you had asked a Cleanthes: But where in the universe would you expect to find this designer either still at work or contemplating his work and calling it good? I suppose he would have said: Don't be too literal-minded: we cannot understand God well enough to know what the words mean. But he would have evidence enough from the design we have discovered and go on discovering.

Is the view of Cleanthes science or isn't it? Is the designer the primitive substance from which all that we know of the universe has developed? Is the designer the first all of things we can have any knowledge of, having a place within the natural world? Hume is prepared to consider this as a hypothesis: he suggests that there may have been at some stage a contriving mind, but that we have no reason to say that it is primordial: it must have developed from some still earlier substance. This he can suggest because he regards even the most complex organism (in this case the mind of the contriver) as a possible growth out of more primitive materials. But it is easy to see that if he *can* consider the sequence: primitive substance: designer: minds, animals, organisms, systems: then he has no particular reason for introducing the designer. He can, instead, argue that minds and other known organisms evolved from more primitive systems without the help of a designing intelligence. The only particular reason he could have for introducing the designer would be some evidence that cannot be interpreted otherwise.

And if the view of Cleanthes is not science, what is it? It is what Hume called philosophy incorporating itself with a system of theology.[1] It is not an attempt to explain what we observe of nature by hypotheses about nature: but to explain *all* nature by reference to a being entirely

[1] *The Natural History of Religion*, §11.

outside nature. Hume's own method of enquiry could have led him to the view that hydrogen atoms are the primitive substance from which all that we have so far observed has issued. That could not be the conclusion reached by a philosophy which had incorporated itself with a system of theology.

My conclusion is that a purely theoretical enquiry into the natural world and its origins is an enquiry into formal–efficient causes within nature. Of course this reveals intelligences operating by final causes—ourselves certainly and animals almost certainly. But enquiry into origins traces people and animals back to simpler forms of life and so to inanimate matter. No intelligent agency is revealed on any larger scale and none is primitive. The attempt to identify such cosmic intelligences is certainly not now a scientific undertaking. This is because in such an undertaking considerations are allowed to count which would be excluded from a scientific enquiry. These considerations sprang originally from religion.

We may nevertheless ask whether the discovery of a cosmic contriver of order in the universe is a discovery which would help us to understand the meaning of it all. If the First Cause were Efficient–Formal and Final Cause at once, would our knowledge of it answer the question: 'What is it all in aid of? How ought we to live? Why am I here?'

Hume decides *not*. So far as we know the plan, this will of course be useful to us: it will enable us to forecast events in nature, including the actions of other people.

PHILOSOPHY AND THE MEANING OF LIFE

But we are in no way obliged to *like* the plan: it will certainly not be designed for our personal advantage. We can perhaps best adopt an attitude of acquiescence, but we need not do so. Nothing we do can please or displease God. On this view, the greatest intelligence and the most powerful will may be unavoidably required to explain the world as a going concern. But what we have to take note of in our lives is the world itself and the way it works. A wise man is guided by what he believes the world to be: above all by what he believes about his fellow men and his own society. This is as it is because God so ordered it: but this view of its origin does nothing to enhance its practical importance. Our only 'duty' to God is to assert that he exists if we believe it. (A curious duty which I suppose we also owe to Mount Everest.) What we know of God cannot in itself lead us to do or forbear to do any action.

The philosophy incorporating into itself a system of theology decides quite differently. It proposes to infer from the part of the world open to our observation that God loves and cares for all his creatures and has a plan for the good of each. If the actual evidence seems to show that God cares for only some of his creatures, willingly sacrifices some for the good of others, this is because we cannot know the whole of the plan. If it seems that the contrivance of nature is incomplete or even botched and clumsy; that creatures are sacrificed for no good at all: this must not lead us to conclude that God is imperfect either in intelligence or power or love. Could we understand the whole plan (which in our present state we

THE FIRST QUESTION

cannot ever expect to do) we should see how everything
is planned for a consummation of good for all. This of
course is where the theological system shows most clearly.
If the concept of God as First Cause (efficient or final) were
an hypothesis accepted simply as explaining the world we
know, we must construct God's character and attributes
from the world as we experience it. We would never be
entitled to go beyond what the evidence requires. Did the
world seem perfect to us from our experience and observation, we must infer a like perfection in God. Since it
appears imperfect we cannot do so. Hume clearly saw
that the concept of a perfect God is not a scientific concept, designed to explain the facts. It is an idea that
intrudes from elsewhere—from traditional religions and
theology.

It would be argued by many theologians that they are in a
position to draw more positive conclusions than Hume
because they conder sievidence which he excluded. This
might be put in fairly crude terms: the evidence of benign
miracles. It is not difficult to see that Hume would (and
did) find many other ways of accounting for such miracles
as well as many opportunities for introducing malign
miracles into the argument. But the point about wider
evidence can be put less crudely. Theologians might claim
that Hume has too narrow a concept of experience: omits
mystical experience; omits the sense of good that comes to
men particularly in adversity; omits men's need for spiritual help and daily bread, their sense of sin and need for
forgiveness.

121

Certainly Hume had a simple and narrow view of human nature, but if we try to add what he omitted from the evidence, will it not show much to be counted on both sides of the balance? That the human needs which Hume neglected are often *not* met: that the goods he overlooked are often available only at overwhelming cost to the beneficiary or to others?

It seems to me that Hume was correct in arguing in his other great work *The Natural History of Religion* that theological conceptions can be understood only by reference to human living and practice. That practical considerations often impinge upon theoretical enquiries is obvious enough. A student abandons one problem because he finds somebody who will pay him for undertaking a different one. A scientist publishes his views not because he is now sure they are correct but because he is now sure he has little time to live. These cases suggest nothing in the way of intellectual dishonesty. Other examples do suggest this: a discovery is not published because it interferes with some industrial interest: or because it would be condemned by the Pope or the king or regarded as nonsense by the Fellows of the Royal Society. And statements are made for the converse reasons. It would be idle to question that this second thing has often happened where scientific enquiry has been under the control of church or state or other powerful institutions. Hume was not wrong to treat the theories of theologians with reserve.

However, what I am after is a more fundamental connexion. There are tight corners in which it is defensible and reasonable to adopt beliefs for which there is very

little evidence.[1] Suppose afterwards we might, if we so
decided, take another long look at these beliefs and the
evidence for and against them: does it not often happen
that we merely stick to what we originally said? And by
that time many other people may have accepted their
beliefs from us without criticism. And of course the
opportunity to re-examine the evidence may not in fact
occur. In some such ways, I feel sure, the hazards of
practice give rise to beliefs—often held most tenaciously;
beliefs which survive long after the occasion of their
adoption has been forgotten. One can add, of course, that
since many different people find themselves in the same
sorts of dilemmas and fixes, what has served one may
continue to serve others. Of course it may be that many
such beliefs are really rational: there is (had we the
occasion to examine it) good evidence for them. But
some will not be so. I shall argue that it is not *necessarily*
either dishonest or unreasonable to cling to irrational
beliefs.

Finally it must be added that we have concepts which
are framed for practice but get used in theory: these give
rise to the more puzzling kinds of statement. For instance,
we might speak of a powerful feeling which arises in us
when we see a cataract or stand beneath an overhanging
crag: it is a *power*. And we might on some other occasion
use this notion of power to explain events which occur
there—an accident or a suicide. We see what gradations
and ambiguities are possible. Hume remarks that copula-
tion, 'suitably to the importance and dignity of it, was

[1] See Chapter 7, pp. 169–71; Chapter 9, pp. 194–203.

divided among several deities.'[1] This subdivision is a reflexion of man's mounting anxiety: if placating one god does not work, try several. But it connects also with explaining processes as experience and analysis brings unexpected complexity to light. In Hesiod's time there were 30,000 deities: each was or had been of practical importance, a mode of operating in one world: but this number was found to be insufficient for 'the task to be performed'. Because what is thought of as a mode of operating or effecting a change is also thought of as explaining the same change when it occurs without or against our will. My main point is that we might try in this way to understand the intrusion of religious concepts into scientific explanations.

The conclusion of this chapter is that if we ask about the First Cause of the world in a purely theoretical spirit, then the answer must be sought along the lines of science (which are not new but older than Christianity). The enquiry becomes many enquiries and the methods of tackling them become very technical. The answers are often highly debatable: the margins of error may be enormous. But the answers give us only formal-efficient causes, not final causes.

The objection might be made that scientific procedures are not the only ones by which people try to answer theoretical questions about nature. This of course is true.[2]

[1] *The Natural History of Religion*, §2, note.
[2] See Hume's own unguarded gesture towards explaining events by reference to gods: *The Natural History of Religion*, §11. He concludes: 'The whole mythological system is so natural, that, in the vast

And even if we could show that other procedures have been introduced on account of confusion or even fraud, it would not *prove* that these other procedures have no real use or validity. If science has the orthodox methods of the age, this does not entail that unorthodox methods are totally mistaken. The history of science shows that our ideas of method have changed. And in any age the unorthodox enquirer is entitled to some sort of hearing.

variety of planets and worlds, contained in this universe, it seems more than probable, that, somewhere or other, it is really carried into execution.'

CHAPTER 6

MYSELF AND THE WORLD

❖◇❖◇❖◇❖◇❖◇❖◇❖◇❖◇❖◇❖◇❖◇❖◇❖◇❖◇❖◇❖◇❖◇❖◇❖

THE FIRST QUESTION, What is the meaning of the world? presupposes that there are people for whom the world could have meaning. The meaning is for somebody. If nobody (no person) had ever lived, the world would have had a character, a history and duration, and perhaps also an order and direction, but no meaning. If there were nobody, the world's history and duration would not be known but they would be there: no meaning would be there.[1] The second question, What is the point or reason for my own existence? presupposes not merely somebody to be interested in such questions of meaning, but someone whose life may itself have a meaning. The question assumes a distinction between myself and the rest of the world. Why am I included in the world? Granted that there is a world, why did it have to include me? In this chapter I mean to tackle some questions about the identity and existence of a person. How do I know who I am? How do I distinguish myself from the rest of the world? Might I have been somebody else? Unless I know who I am, how can I decide whether life has a meaning for me? And if I have doubts about who I am or whether I really exist, then it is unlikely that I shall discover any meaning in life at all.

[1] Compare Wittgenstein: *Tractatus Logico-Philosophicus*, 6.41.

These questions are partly logical or philosophical. I naturally ask: How can I be sure that I exist? because there is a corresponding question about other people. How can I be sure that Lyndon B. Johnson exists? In the case of other people there are generally recognised methods for making sure and a pretty clear standard of what is a reasonable assurance. I could, if I had to, say exactly why I am sure that Lyndon B. Johnson exists. May I not ask the same question about anyone—about myself? And here the puzzle is that I always would assert and never deny my own existence: I do not have to search about to make sure that I have identified the right person and not somebody else. And although I am so sure, I should not find it at all easy to explain just how I made sure.

We sometimes ask: But might he not have been somebody else? I can therefore ask: Might I not have been somebody else? And here the puzzling thing is that I do not easily decide whether the answer ought to be yes or no: and how am I to decide? This logical puzzle can connect with a question of a rather different kind: suppose my father had married somebody else? And the question: Might I become somebody else? can seem vaguely threatening as well as bewildering.

The philosophical puzzles are tackled by trying to make clear the logical relationships between different statements and questions; setting them side by side and showing how they are alike and how they differ; examining the expressions and their use in different contexts. Some philosophers hold that this method does not go all the way: that all the clarification that can be offered leaves us with unanswered questions—and this above all when we are concerned with the relationship between myself and the external world. Some of these still-remaining questions are discussed in Chapter 8.

The philosophical questions might occur to anybody: but there are also questions that arise for people who are in difficulty with themselves. For example a man may want to reject himself. How is that done? These special questions connect with the logical puzzles: quite elementary logical questions can, in susceptible people, give rise to acute dread or panic. And I think that some of the emotional misgivings people have about themselves and the world are sometimes made worse by confusions of a logical kind. In examining the connexion between knowing who I am, and discovering a meaning in my life, both sorts of questions arise. I shall deal with logical questions on pages 128–41; on pages 141–6 with some of the psychological conditions which lead people to ask questions about themselves; and on pages 146–53 I consider some rather wild accounts of myself and the world—accounts which seem to me to be attempts to express and even to systematise very disorientated views of the world.

How do I know that I exist? How do I know who I am? These questions refer to the *numerical identity* of a certain person. They are not about what sort of person I am, but about *which* person I am. I may also ask: How do I know what sort of person I am—and *do I know*? First consider how these two questions, of numerical identity and of sort or character, are asked about anybody.

I ask about someone: Who is he? An answer might give his name, John Smith, on the assumption that we can in this way distinguish him from everybody else who might come into the picture. Another answer might be: This is the man who wrote to you from Los Angeles. This of course is a description and it could apply to dozens of people—if I had dozens of correspondents in Los Angeles. But it can very well serve as what philosophers call a *definite description*; that is, it may serve to distinguish him for me from everybody else just because in fact nobody else has written to me from Los Angeles. If so, it serves to establish for me his numerical identity: it says which person he is. I may then go on to ask what kind of person he is—young or old, friendly or hostile?

Compare this with a different situation. Seeing someone in my room, I ask: Is this the same person who came last week? This certainly asks a question about numerical identity: never mind whether he is of the same kind, is he in fact the same individual? A person may change in many ways without ceasing to be the same individual.

We ask corresponding questions about things and animals. Is my watch the same watch I received as a wedding present? The face and hands are not the same: the glass, strap and ratchet have been renewed again and again: and in fact all the inside mechanism is new. Can it still be the same watch? What we reply depends on how we use the word 'watch'. Questions of numerical identity are always of the form: Is this the same so-and-so? where 'so-and-so' stands for a certain *sort* of thing— a watch, a house, a book, a dog. We can answer such a question only if we know the meaning of 'watch', 'house' etc. We know the meaning well enough if we know how it is to be used in this sort of context. The degree of precision needed depends upon the sort of business we are at when the question is asked.

When I ask about a person: Is he the same individual person I came across last week? the answer can be given only if we know how the word 'person' is to be understood. And how can I be sure that I am the same person who was given the watch on his wedding day? In many ways I know I am a different sort of person: but a person (like a watch or a book or a house) can become a different sort of person without becoming a different person. Just what changes are *not* compatible with being the same person? Should I ever say that I had become a different person?

I have set the question about my own continuing identity over against the question about the identity of someone I meet. In the second case I may at once admit that I do not know whether this is the same person or not. But what can I say of myself? *We want to say:* I always know who I am, I can always distinguish myself from anybody else: I always know that I exist, that the world includes me. If we are so sure, how are we sure?

Compare this talk about myself with parallel talk about 'you'. Do I not also always know that you exist, always distinguish you from other people, always know who you are? When I address you, I do not say: Please if you exist, will you tell me the time. I know you are, and must be, you. And if I were to ask Do you exist? Why does the world have to include you? I should be astonished to hear you reply: Well as a matter of fact I do not exist, the world does not include me.

It might be objected that this is a verbal trick: it all depends on using the pronoun 'you'. If in place of 'you' I said 'John Smith', then why should I be so sure that John Smith exists? I might not know at all: I might confuse John Smith with somebody else: and I could indeed say: John Smith, if he exists, is to tell me the time. And is not the same true about my existence? If for 'I', I substitute 'K.B.', then why must I know that K.B. exists? Might I not doubt it? Might I not confuse K.B. with John Smith?

Certainly it is true of both the original formulations (about 'me' and about 'you') that their special feature depends on the use of these pronouns—their primary use in face-to-face conversations. The pronouns are used to identify the speaker and the person he addresses. The speaker says: I would like you to tell me the time. The words are or are intended to be addressed to somebody. I should not in the same sense use 'you' if I perceived nobody to be addressed. And in my opinion the primary point of both 'you' and 'I' is to draw the attention *of the hearer* to the fact that I am speaking to him. The words serve to identify me as the speaker and to indicate that he, my audience, is the one who is to reply. They *identify me* to the hearer: he could afterwards recount it as 'The man in the grey suit spoke to me'. The words do not identify the hearer to the hearer: how could that be necessary? They simply indicate that he and not anyone else is to make reply. We could say that 'I' draws the hearer's attention to the speaker's existence: but not that 'you' draws the hearer's attention to his own existence. But what both words do, they do for *the hearer*.

What do the pronouns do for the speaker? The use of 'you' does not serve to identify the hearer to the speaker. This has already been done: it is because the speaker has seen and picked out the hearer that he asks him the time. Nor does the use of 'I' serve to identify the speaker to himself: how could that be necessary? Consider the case where, hearing a noise, I call out: You there, I want you to come out. If nobody is there I cannot identify myself to him, nor indicate to him that he is the one to come out. My words do not in fact refer anybody to anybody. I only use 'you' because I believe I have already identified somebody—'the man making that noise'. But the description applies to nobody. I only use 'I' to attract the attention of 'the man behind the wall': and there is nobody behind the wall.

I am arguing that my use of 'you' shows that I am making an assumption or holding a belief which may be false—because there may be nobody there to be addressed. And I could call out: Why do you exist? Why does the world include you? and get no answer. But my use of 'I' does not involve an assumption of a parallel kind: in order to speak I do not even have to jump to the conclusion that I exist.

This account is contrary to the view of Descartes. He argued that his use of 'I' in 'I think', involves an assumption: and his famous deduction, 'I think, therefore I am', was intended to make an implicit assumption explicit. And of course the extraordinary thing about Descartes's assumption is that it cannot be wrong. In effect Descartes takes his use of 'I' as serving to identify himself to *himself* rather than to his audience, if any.[1]

If I use 'you' or refer to 'John Smith' I show that I have made a claim that could be false. I can be asked how I know that John Smith is there, or that there is somebody listening to me. Such claims can be supported by evidence: and what would my evidence be? I see him, I see somebody, or I hear him, or I remember seeing him. I may introduce myself to other people by a name or a description. I am K.B. or I am the owner of this house. And I can properly be asked to prove it. How shall I offer my evidence? In the long run I shall have to rely on what I have seen or heard and now remember—or on things which I now see and show you. I do this to convince others that I am the person called K.B. or the owner of this house. But I do not identify myself to myself in this sort of way. On the contrary I say: I see, I remember—and not 'a person of a certain description sees or remembers'. If 'I remember' meant 'A person of a certain description remembers', then it would be a question how was I sure that there was anyone answering to that description (a question to be answered presumably by reference to what I see or remember). When I say I remember I do not even claim to be 'the person who remembers'. If I made that claim I might be asked: Are you sure it is you who remembers and not somebody

---

[1] *Discourse on Method*, iv.

else? When I say I remember (or I see, I hear, etc.) I claim *to remember*. And I cannot be asked how I know I remember or how I know that I see or hear.[1]

I have been discussing face-to-face speech situations. We also use language in writing—to people who are absent, to people we have never met, to people who may not exist. I shall not discuss this complication. We also spend much time talking to ourselves—asking ourselves questions and offering ourselves answers. It seems to me that this conversation with oneself is a derivative use of speech: we use the language we have learned to speak with others. But the question arises, if I ask myself: Is he the man I met in Venice in 1958? what use has 'he' and what use has 'I'? In speech I need 'I' to refer the hearer to me, and 'he' to refer the hearer to a third person. What do I need them for when I am thinking, not speaking to anybody?

First of all I do this often as a preparation for speech. We often want to choose which expression to use when the occasion arises. But I do it also for a second important reason. I need to formulate what I am believing or wondering: for example I need to ask myself whether he or I was responsible for an accident: and to do this I have to distinguish very clearly everything that I did and everything that he did. This may lead me to *feel* that I was at fault.

Could I not have this feeling without expressing anything in language? Could I not simply feel guilty or

[1] See Sydney Shoemaker: *Self-Knowledge and Self-Identity* and S. Coval: *Scepticism and the First Person*.

ashamed? Surely there are feelings that need no language: I can feel pain or grief without telling myself what I feel.

I think the answer is that some feelings are not possible without the use of language. How, except in language, am I to feel remorse that I passed another car at the wrong point? Other feelings, many of which we share with animals, can be wordless.[1] But if we use speech to ourselves, it is the speech we use with others: we speak *as if* to another and the difference between the use of 'he' and the use of 'I' is the same in both modes. We give each its proper place.

Talking to ourselves can be compared with writing for ourselves or drawing diagrams. Why do we use pen and paper when things get complicated? To keep them in their 'proper places'. What makes a place on a piece of paper, the proper place? A language-writing system. For example, we *begin* reading at the top left-hand corner: that is what *comes first*. The correctness is correctness in a system of rules. And of course writing presupposes the system of speech: including the place of 'you' and the place of 'I'.

In thought I may refer to myself by name or description—but if the name or description were inapplicable then I could become convinced of it. I could ask myself: How do you know you are called K.B.? How do you know you were born in the North Riding? And I could be expected to say how I know. I should do it by citing what I have seen or heard or remembered and this might or might not be conclusive evidence. But I cannot be asked how I know that I see or hear or remember.

[1] See Wittgenstein: *Philosophical Investigations*, Part II, §1.

I can say of somebody else: He is not the person I thought: and this can carry the implication: But someone else is. For example; He is not the author of this book—but somebody else is. I can also say: He might have been the author—but was not. What does it mean to say that a person is or might have been different? And can I ask the same sort of questions about myself?

There is no difficulty in supposing that anyone (myself included) might have been of a different sort—taller or kinder or braver. The difficulty begins when we have what purports to be a definite description—one that can apply to only one person—and he is known *only* by description. Here we often use a proper name—Napoleon —as a shorthand for a definite description: the man who was First Emperor of the French, lost the Battle of Waterloo, died on St. Helena. It must make sense to say that Napoleon (who lost Waterloo) might have won it. If he had, the name 'Napoleon' would not have had this connotation, but would still have had others. Of course Napoleon might never have been born: but in that case we should have to abandon every description of him. There is nothing to suggest that if Napoleon had won at Waterloo he would have been a different person: certainly he could not have been Wellington. And the historian who says: The prisoner of St. Helena might have been somebody else, only means that he cannot make up his mind.[1]

[1] See Bernard Williams : 'Imagination and the self', British Academy Lecture 1966: I can certainly imagine myself being somebody else —Napoleon for example. Professor Williams likens this to *acting*

The way we talk about other people gives us little encouragement to say that one person might have been or is somebody else. Could you have been somebody else? By using 'you' I indicate that I believe I have identified an audience. I am mistaken if there is nobody there: and then it is certainly not you that is nobody or somebody else.

Could I have been somebody else? Could I have been the person you met in Venice? This description may be definite enough to fit somebody but not in fact me. I may fraudulently claim to be that somebody: I am in a sense claiming to be some other person. But I claim that person is me: that I am what I am, the person you met in Venice. But in fact there are two people involved: the one you met and the one who wrongly claims to be the one you met. If I *remember* meeting you in Venice, my claim is not that I am the one to remember and nobody else is. I do not claim to *be* anybody in particular: I only claim that I remember meeting you: I do not offer any description of *myself* that might be false.

Could I then have been somebody else? If I ask this question about myself I am able to say: I see this and hear that, and remember various things. I cannot be asked how I know that I see or hear or remember: I cannot be asked how I know that it is me and not somebody else who remembers. There is then something about myself I

Napoleon or *pretending* to be Napoleon. In this situation there remain two people: Napoleon and myself (doing the pretending or imagining). But 'although I can certainly imagine being Napoleon . . . I still do not understand, and could not possibly understand, what it would be for me to have been Napoleon' (p. 124).

cannot doubt. Even if I had been different *in kind*, in age or sex, name or nationality or even parentage, I should have to say that I see and hear and remember. If I had been different in kind I should not have been a different person —a different individual. Nor could I become a different person—I began and I shall end. I might so change that others said I was a different person: they would be mistaken.

The problem is not how other people know who I am. They may not know: they can find out by their own observations or by asking me. I may try to explain who I am by offering a definite description of myself which distinguishes me from other people. If they doubt my account they can ask me to offer evidence.

The problem is how I know who I am. What is it that I know that others cannot know in the same way? I offer evidence for what I believe in terms of what I perceive and remember. 'I see trees in the park' is of course about what there is in the park and cannot be true unless there are trees to be seen there. But I am the one who claims to see. Most likely it will make no difference at all to the trees whether I see them or not: it is *to me* that it makes a difference. So also my remembering is a claim about the world and could be false: but I am the one who claims to remember. It makes no difference to the past whether I remember or not. It makes a difference to me. What is not put in question in my claims to perceive or remember —this shows who I am. What is put in question—whether there really are trees to be seen or a visit to Venice to remember—belongs to the outer world of common experience.

As it makes a difference *to me* that I claim to see or to remember, so it makes a difference to me how I feel towards what I claim to perceive or remember. It matters to me: it may well make no difference at all to the object I claim to see or to have seen. A person is one who feels about what he claims to see of the world: or who suffers pain as well as damage. The damage is there for all to see: I can feel pain and conceal it from others. It makes no sense to speak of concealing it from myself. One who feels pain does not first of all have to ask himself: Am I the one who feels pain or is it somebody else?

The division, marked in grammar or logic, between myself and the world, incorporates two fundamental features. (1) Different speakers are taken to be referring in speech to the same objects and events. This is in fact something we are in general able to do. It puts some things (chairs and tables, mountains and stars, all living creatures including men and women) into the world-outside-me. If there is to be a division there must be things that fall fairly and squarely on one side or the other: there must be a real self and a real objective world. And this objective world is established by a language we share with other people. I take the sounds they make to be speech: their statements to be testimony which is independent of my own perceptions. If I did not, I should not regard what they say as either confirmation or refutation of what I say myself. So that the speech we share defines the common world,

> the very world which is the world
> Of all of us—the place where, in the end,
> We find our happiness, or not at all.[1]

(2) Different speakers are taken to be seeing, hearing, remembering, enjoying or suffering pain. People are not merely mines of information about the public world: they are also persons. I have all sorts of ways of identifying another person: obviously my fundamental method is that he is a large mobile solid—continuous in motion or rest; but this is not all—he cannot be divided although his body can. So that a person is not simply a body. He is one who claims to see, hear, remember, enjoy or suffer. I take his experiences to be *real*. Hume considers the case of one who is a spectator of one of the more terrible operations of surgery. The spectator is not being hurt in one sense: the pain of the victim can never be his pain: yet the spectator also suffers. This is part of what we mean when we say that we regard other people as having real experiences.[2]

It is one of the paradoxes of life that we all live alongside each other in the public world: but our private worlds are in some respects worlds apart. So that, while for me the world of childhood belongs to the remote past, I have to remember that this same world (or one very much like it) still exists alongside the afternoon world and the evening

---

[1] Wordsworth: *The Prelude*, Book XI, 142 f. The common world is discussed further in Chapter 8 below.

[2] See Wittgenstein: *Philosophical Investigations*, Part I, §265, 270 etc., and Hume: *Treatise of Human Nature*, Book III, Part iii, §1.

world. This reflects the contrasts of public and private. The far-away pre-historic world of childhood still exists, much as you remember it perhaps: although it will never be your world again. In the public world the clock marches on, hardly noticing the quite different cycle of changes in our own lives.

There is then a real world we share and a real self. And of course there is also the unreal: we make mistakes, we see a post as a tree, a coat as a man. Any claim we make about the external world might be mistaken. If there were no persons there would be no mistakes, nothing would be imaginary or illusory. But nothing would be seen or known either.

The preceding discussion has been about the questions: What am I? Why cannot I doubt that I really exist? I have dealt with these questions from a logical point of view. Logic is the grammar of normal adult speech: not the grammar of English or French or Chinese but of what could be said in any of these languages and translated into any other. The logic of speech has to be learned and may be forgotten or abandoned under stress. I shall now consider some of the psychological contexts in which these questions are often asked, and where there seems to be a connexion between the context and the answer offered.

(1) Children learn to make a distinction between themselves and the external world long before they learn to talk. But learning our speech tends to emphasise this boundary. The logic of language may be a help: a child may recognise that differences of speech-forms reflect

distinctions he already acknowledges. But even so he has to learn this grammar and this is done partly by 'trying out' possible formulae to see if they are or are not understood by the mother. Clearly the logic of the language could be a great nuisance; it may enforce distinctions in a way which seems strange to the child. There is a right time for each child to learn to talk as well as to learn to walk. But learning to talk shades off into games: a child's new-speech amuses and endears. And even if some day children must learn to talk to a wider audience, and to say what they 'really mean', there is still the realm of fantasy.

Learning to make the distinction involves at some stage a recognition of oneself. Consider the case of Emily Bas-Thornton, aged ten, who climbed to the top of a mast in a pirate ship after having a revelation: it suddenly flashed into her mind that she was *she*. She went on to consider the implications of this fact.

First, what agency had so ordered it that out of all the people in the world who she might have been, she was this particular one, this Emily, born in such-and-such a year out of all the years in Time, . . . Had she chosen herself or had God done it?

How could she have lived ten years without noticing the obvious fact that she was Emily? Did anyone else know that she was some one in particular, not just any little girl? She for the first time had a feeling of being quite distinct from her brothers and sisters—they were now as separate from her as the ship itself. And she also wondered if perhaps she was herself God: and reflected that if she were she must be able to perform miracles. She decided it would be easier to deal with that situation when she was older. The whole experience was frightening and she determined to keep all her discoveries and doubts to herself.[1]

(2) People may lose what is often called 'a sense of their own reality'. This can come and go: in some contexts it is clear, in others not at all clear. (Obviously this is one of the questions at issue in early childhood.) If I do not feel sure of myself I do not feel sure of the boundary. Some things in the world seem much less real than others. Feeling oneself to be unreal may take the form of seeming to see oneself as one external object among many—as so often in dreams. And it connects with the feeling that one can predict one's own actions but not make up one's own mind. John Stuart Mill's *Autobiography* shows a philosopher in this state at the age of twenty. In such a condition the logic of our language and the way of life it structures can be an added burden. All that people say of me presupposes that I am real and I cannot feel real. As in the first example, it is my numerical identity that seems to be at issue: who do people mean when they talk of me? May I not really be somebody else? Am I anything at all?

Logicians find these questions very confused. How can reality be a matter of degree? The logician would prefer to interpret the statement: 'This does not seem altogether real' as 'I am not altogether sure that this is real'. ('This does not seem altogether square' may mean 'I am not quite sure that it is square': but of course it could mean 'The sides are not quite equal'.) If people are real, does it

[1] Richard Hughes: *A High Wind in Jamaica*, Chapter 6.

matter that they do not always feel it? Do animals or trees or stars feel real? So that the logician's view may well be that anyone who says (as many people do say and no doubt many more would like to say) that they feel unreal, must be real if what they say is true or even untrue: and perhaps what they mean is that they do not feel themselves to be important or significant in the way they are expected to be. We can certainly connect the feeling of reality with the feeling of responsibility.[1] We so use language that there seems no way of avoiding the conclusion that I (as a real person) am responsible for my own opinions, decisions and actions. And I may not *feel* responsible for them: I may feel that nobody is responsible for them or that somebody else is. Mill seems to have thought that for all that he believed and all that he did his father was responsible.

(3) People are naturally unsure about what *kind* of person they are. We none of us have complete knowledge of what kind of person we are: but the ignorance and uncertainty may in youth go very deep. One may wonder whether one is sane or mad, homosexual or heterosexual; whether one's fantasies are natural or unnatural. This question connects with the previous two and is easily confused with them. It turns on my character, not my numerical identity: but when we question the numerical identity of some other person or thing we of course use character as a test. And it is highly symptomatic that in states of crisis and confusion one asks questions about

[1] Compare Wordsworth in *The Prelude* and in *Tintern Abbey* where he gives an account of a shifting boundary between what we perceive and what we 'half create'.

oneself as if they were questions about another person. I seem to see myself as an object and a questionable object: I become embarrassed about my name and about what I see in the mirror.

This last question has a further complication. I ask what kind of person I am but I know that to some extent this is a matter for me to decide. I ask what is to become of me or what I am to become, as well as what I am. Even where I would claim to know what I am, I may wonder what I will become. 'We know what we are, we know not what we may be.' So that this is a question of aim as well as of present fact: the doubt may be a hesitation of the will— something to be determined rather than discovered. And I may both seem able to predict my own future and at the same time be unable to avoid facing a decision which could falsify my prediction. I may predict failure but still not avoid having to make a decision whether to go on or to give up.

To separate these questions completely from each other is impossible. One might say that the first two raise questions of antecedent causes, the third, of aims. The first two connect with the question: Where did I come from—why me and not somebody else? Here there is a simple answer: Two people were joined and produced a third according to well-known laws of nature. This often fails to satisfy. It may not seem to explain me as a person separate from my parents, or—perhaps not very reason-ably—from one of them; or not to explain me as separate from my brothers and sisters—or from one of them. So it leaves me with the feeling of not quite being a real person.

Or the type of explanation may seem inappropriate: I am reluctant to accept the view that something real could come from a world accidentally churning out people and things according to its rule not mine. I feel this does not make me as real as I ought to be: I am unwilling to admit that I am not the world.

The third question concerns the purpose or end for the sake of which my existence was brought about. Is there some overall end to be served, and if so can I find out what it is? Will it give me a purpose in my life, a good reason for becoming a certain sort of person? Am I free to follow it or to reject it? This of course is a practical question.

It is ideally possible to distinguish between philosophical doubt about myself and the world, and what is sometimes called 'pathological doubt'. The first is an extension of commonsense reflection, even if the results arrived at give a new look to commonsense beliefs. The second tends to reject commonsense beliefs outright. The first is a logical examination of the grounds of ordinary beliefs. It often leads us to acknowledge that the grounds are not at all what we had taken them to be. In particular, philosophers have often tried to show that many things we suppose can be proved cannot be proved at all and so might be untrue. What do they want us to do about it? It is rare for philosophers to conclude that we simply ought not to go on holding such beliefs. Their enquiries seldom bring out any good reasons for holding that the beliefs are in fact *untrue*. The more usual conclusion is that we should recognise new and different considerations as being good grounds for belief: or that the beliefs should be accepted as 'natural'. After all, our general beliefs about ourselves and the world are not to be abandoned lightly. They are, as Hume said, 'the foundation of all our thoughts and actions, so that upon their removal human nature must immediately perish and go to ruin'.[1]

However it is by no means always possible to make this distinction between philosophical questioning and pathological doubt. I shall consider several more or less systematic views about the reality of myself and of the external world which seem to me either borderline or well over the border. One derives from a philosopher: it is not in fact a position to which in the end he adheres. In other cases, the doubts formulated connect with particular emotional states. All of them seem to me to be incoherent and unworkable but not all of them are obviously refutable.

(1) Descartes begins with the very proper notion that when I claim to perceive or to remember, I am sometimes mistaken. Can I then go on to doubt whether I ever perceive anything or remember anything? Could the whole external world which I ordinarily believe I perceive, be a complete illusion?[2]

As we have seen, Descartes was anxious to discover whether there was anything, 'of all he formerly believed' which he could not doubt: and came to the conclusion that he could not doubt his own existence. But he could

[1] *Treatise of Human Nature*, Book I, Part iv, §4.
[2] *Discourse on Method*, IV.

still doubt whether the external world existed—including his own body and all other people. This is his position at a crucial stage of his argument. I want to ask whether it makes sense.

'I myself am real but the external world is not real.' Is it possible to discover evidence that contradicts this view? A person endowed with the usual senses and ability could use his eyes and ears and memory and in doing so might discover that he can learn from the actions and speech of other people. What he learns in this way, he will not interpret as being about what other people see or hear or remember, but about what he himself would see or hear or remember if he stood where they stand, or had moved about the world as the speakers have done. What he learns he will not even interpret as the evidence of his own senses: a man does not need to believe that he has eyes in order to see, ears in order to hear: and we all remember without having any particular beliefs about how we remember. For such a man nothing would really exist of the physical world except what he 'sees,' 'hears' and 'remembers'. (Nothing would count for him as an actual perceiving or remembering because he would say that there is nothing there to be perceived or remembered.)

This view really places nothing at all on the far side of the boundary between myself and the world. For one who takes this view there really is no boundary: so that the concept of *myself* is not used to distinguish anything from anything: it is really as empty for him as the concept of an external world. For Descartes this is only a stage in an argument. He goes on to offer new arguments for the reality of the external world. The world is after all really there because God put it there and keeps it there. We may after all believe in general in the evidence of our senses and our memory. What would Descartes have done if he had not made this appeal to God? It seems very likely that the view he took as a stage in an argument is a view that some people have to try to live with.

(2) This suggests a consideration of the converse view: 'I myself am not real: but the external world, including other people, is real'. How would this differ from the world as we ordinarily take it? There are trees in the park, voices in my room, and I (who claim to be unreal) say that I see and hear them. Other people will say: 'He sees' or 'He remembers' and will be prepared to describe the person they claim to be speaking about. But perhaps when they say these things they are mistaken. Somebody takes me to have asked a question: this appears when he answers it. But it could be that on this occasion he mistook the situation and I did not ask him a question. Obviously it can sometimes happen that people are mistaken in thinking I am there and that I say I have seen or re-membered something. Can this be generalised: whenever people think I am there saying things, I am not there. Obviously the world could contain some sort of machine that was regularly mistaken by other people for a person: they would think of it as a real person—but mistakenly.

What should we say of someone who said: Yes, that is the situation and that 'person' who is *never* there is me. What would people think if I set out to prove that *nobody* put the lights out last night—and added: I put them out.

If anyone holds this view we can ask him if he believes it. If he agrees that he believes it we can ask on what grounds he believes it: and we can point out that the only grounds he could have must be something he himself sees or hears or remembers. At this point I suspect he might offer some sort of evidence: about how he feels, how people behave as if he did not exist, about how he does not know what to make of himself. I have already referred to such evidence. In the meantime we would perhaps conclude that the man has something to say but cannot say it without misusing our language. It is as though he wants to put nothing on the near side of the boundary between himself and the external world: so that for him, as for the first sceptic, there is no boundary.[1]

Both these views face the great difficulty that their case can be expressed (if at all) only in a language which only one person uses. And I think there are grave doubts whether in such a language there is any real distinction between truth and falsehood.[2] In the first example, who is to confirm my statements about 'seeing' and 're-

[1] See A. J. Ayer: *The Problem of Knowledge*, Chapter II. Ayer discusses the possibility that a person might know many things about the world without knowing that he himself existed: he might even know that things were known but not that they were known by him or any other person. This 'whole conception of knowledge would be impersonal'. Ayer says it is not a self-contradictory notion but admits that perhaps it is strange (p. 47). Of course, Ayer is throughout speaking of someone who does not know that he exists, not of someone who denies his own existence.

[2] See Rush Rhees: 'Can there be a Private Language?', *Proceedings of the Aristotelian Society*, Supp. Vol. 28, 1954.

membering': who is to correct me if I am mistaken? Strictly speaking, all my claims to see or remember any external object must on this view be mistaken: nor can these claims be understood to mean that I 'seem to see' or 'seem to remember', since these phrases get their meaning by contrast with actually seeing trees or re-membering incidents. In the second case there could be a world in which people use language just as we do: but it will not be possible for me to claim to take part in such a language. For, in our language, words are used to describe what people claim to see or hear or remember. And I make no such claim.

Neither view is coherent: but these views may have some importance because they are the sort of thing people sometimes say, whether in trying to express their own views or in trying to describe the states of mind they attribute to others.

(3) I have considered the two extreme cases: the denial of the reality of the external world and the denial of the reality of the self. There are intermediate cases where the speaker seems not to be abolishing the boundary between himself and the external world, but trying to insist upon a different boundary. For example: (i) 'I am real and physical objects are real; other people are just physical objects.' (ii) 'I am real and I include what other people call the mind or self of my mother. She and I are one and the same person: there are other persons and there are things.' (iii) 'There is me and there is what other people some-times call "my other self". People think of us as one person but of course we are two people. To me *he* is just

one of the other people who (along with things) make up the external world.'

If the speaker tries to talk in these ways systematically he will certainly get into trouble with ordinary language. Of course people sometimes make mistakes while intending to observe the ordinary boundaries. And there could be people who in certain moods give up the attempt to observe the boundaries and become for a time very incoherent and obscure. It may sometimes be difficult to decide whether a person has made a mistake or has adopted a different notion of the boundary.

If we stick to the logic of our common language, then my identity is shown by my use of I see, I hear, I remember, I am in pain. In so far as other people recognise me as a person they take my words as evidence: in so far as they recognise me as the same continuing person they cannot accept from me both I see x and I do not see x. Their reasons for identifying me depend of course upon their observations. I show my own continuing identity: and it is not incorrect to say *I know it* so long as it is recognised that I cannot be asked how I know it. This is all fundamental to the working of language. It may still seem mysterious. Certainly it is astonishing that we have a language at all.[1]

For some people, and perhaps for everyone at some stage or other, logic is not enough: they need more reassurance than logic can give about their own reality and the reality of the common world. This leads people to

[1] See Chapter 8 below.

talk of a divine will and intelligence creating the world and ordering its ways: and by a separate fiat creating my soul—which comes not from my parents but from God. It seems as if nothing *can* assure me of my reality, or assure me that I am not the whole of reality, or determine for me how my life fits into the whole, except a being who is totally incommensurable with all created things. While our language makes the distinctions—myself, the world, other persons—we can add: religion attempts to deal with some of the greatest difficulties which people encounter in trying to apply these distinctions or in living with people who apply them. Religion holds things in their proper places by exhibiting God as the centre of the pattern. (So in social life order and degree are justified as a pattern centred upon God, ordained of God, and valid without reference to the personal merit of the high or the low, or their closeness to God.)

This religious attempt does not always succeed. The idea that I myself am God is not uncommon in dreams: children may have it and need to be convinced that they are not omnipotent. It is a familiar symptom of mental disorder. And even Descartes went to the trouble of proving to himself that he was not God.[1]

---

[1] *Discourse on Method*, IV.

CHAPTER 7

PRACTICAL QUESTIONS

❖◇❖◇❖◇❖◇❖◇❖◇❖◇❖◇❖◇❖◇❖◇❖◇❖◇❖◇❖◇❖◇❖◇❖◇❖◇❖

HAVE ALLEGED that at least on one proper interpretation, the question of the meaning of life is a practical question. What distinguishes practical questions from others? I begin by comparing different sorts of questions all of which have some concern with practice or doing.

(1) Questions about doing something in a given situation:

What shall I do for a living?

Whom shall I marry?

How shall I help this wounded man?

What shall I put in my will?

How am I to work harder?

How am I to be revenged on my enemy?

(2) Questions about how this or that kind of action is done:

How do you set a fracture?

How do you fix a life-jacket?

How do you send money overseas?

How do you make friends and influence people?

The first are manifestly practical. The second are really theoretical (and 'universal') in the sense that one can be interested, find out, be well-informed, without any actual practice: and our knowledge can be brought up to date at leisure at any time and need not even have any action at all in view. We can start such a question by naming some end and discovering the means. Even if one experiments, the whole thing is still a matter of coming to know, not of having to do or wanting to do.

We *use* such knowledge as we possess when presented with a situation we believe calls for it, where, as we believe, it could reasonably be applied. But having theoretical skill does not determine what we do on a given occasion. An actual situation has many different features which may call for different actions. So that I may find a broken arm and wonder whether I should set it.

(3) He did everything that should have been done.

He could have tried harder, worked on him longer. These statements are about what *was done* by somebody (perhaps by me) in a given situation. Here again the judgement is unhurried and is open to revision: and one can simply suspend judgement. Making such judgements is (amongst other things) a way of learning what to do and how to do it. If I may have to act in such a situation myself, I must test my skills by watching others, anticipating or remembering what they do, and asking myself and my teachers: Did they do the proper thing? And this, not only in relation to the specialised skills employed: also in relation to the action as a whole—I must consider whether the man who backed out instead of using his specialised skill, was doing the *best thing* in the situation. Here we have the complexity of the actual—something never conveyed in copy-book examples: but the point of my making a judgement on what *was* done is not of course to do something about it myself.

It is answers to the first set of questions that I shall call practical judgements. Here we have to decide what to aim at in *this* situation which, like the doctor's, may be partly or chiefly of our own choosing or, like the Good Samaritan's, the Priest's and the Levite's, definitely not of their own choosing; and how in this situation to try to achieve our aim. We have three things to contend with:

(1) We have many aims and more than one may seem to be at stake in a particular situation: and our notions of what we are aiming at may be fluid and vague.

(2) We have to act on our view of the situation. This generally involves the probabilities as well as what we take to be the actualities of the situation. It is true that if we judge to the best of our abilities we shall be exonerated for our mistakes. But our aim is not to be blameless but to achieve some particular end: and in any case we cannot be blameless if we are content to pretend that we are doing our best: only if we are doing our best. And the question remains: What is best here now?

(3) There is only a limited time in which to act and the time and the problem are not of our own choosing. A refusal (on good or bad grounds) to take any action will itself have foreseeable consequences. Hence a consideration of the importance of a time limit enters into all practical considerations.

I shall examine each of these features of practical judgements.

We have many aims and these may be more or less determinate. Kant supposes that all men have a desire for

their own happiness and presumably this is one of the
aims which lead men to adopt particular ends and so to
practice those specialised techniques which spell out the
means to particular ends. We are *sometimes* guided in our
practical choices by consideration of private happiness but
Kant does not here explain fully how we make the
transition from aiming at happiness to aiming at becoming
a teacher or buying a house at Brighton. And he sees a
difficulty which lies *in the nature of our aim*: happiness
cannot be made definite and so cannot itself give rise to
any single set of technical skills which could be taught or
learned.[1]

How then do we come to adopt particular ends?
Evidently, we adopt some as a means to other ends. Here
Kant explains that one might will to draw intersecting
arcs from the ends of a straight line. Why? Because one
wills to bisect the line and this is (represented as) the
sufficient and necessary means of bisecting a line. But this
would explain why I will to draw the arcs only if it were
sense to say that I *willed* to bisect this line. Why should I
will it? Only as a theoretical exercise could I make it an
end in itself. The 'example' is a stray from pure geometry.

How can it be that I will to become a doctor? Perhaps
because I have to earn a living and I see that this is one way
open to me: I have to choose between the different
possible ways of making a living. At least it is part of the
explanation why I am a doctor, that I make a living that
way. The explanation might be carried further by consideration of my own probable success and happiness in

[1] Kant: *Fundamental Principles of the Metaphysic of Ethics*, p. 41.

this job or that: of my responsibilities to my parents and others. In Kant's view (and I think he is correct) considerations of my own happiness and of other people's are vague and fluctuating but are some of the reasons by which we make up our minds how to earn a living.

Kant regards all technical principles as forms of constraint: I am constrained to work hard and deny myself in order to become a doctor. But of course all my study can be abandoned if only I give up the idea of becoming a doctor. 'We can at any time be free from the precept if we give up the purpose.' I am led by certain considerations to aim and work to become a doctor: but I can do otherwise: *I can at any time change my mind.*[1]

This seems to me very unrealistic. Am I also free at any time to abandon the aim of making a living? Kant holds that it is only a *contingent* fact that other jobs are hard to find: that is to say it is so, but it is perfectly conceivable that it might not have been so. And finally only a contingent fact that (like all men) I desire happiness and not misery: all men *do* desire happiness but one could imagine a man who did not. Kant was unwilling to admit that a rational being is bound by a contingency. A rational being (in his view) is bound by morality which he finds *necessary*—it is so and we cannot conceive it otherwise. This requires very special argument: the fact seems to be that we are all bound and limited precisely by what just happens to be the case.

Once I have become a doctor I have the duties of my

[1] Kant: *Fundamental Principles of the Metaphysic of Ethics*, p. 44.

job to perform. What these are I can in a general way learn at a medical school and from watching other doctors. When faced with a patient, I deliberate as to what is wrong with him and what I can do for him. Aristotle says that a doctor deliberates about means (how to heal) not about ends (whether to heal). As though, because he is a doctor the prior question is somehow settled for him. But what would Aristotle say of the poisoner? How did the poisoner come to find the question of the end settled for him? There is no Royal College of Poisoners: anyone might decide to poison—a doctor might do so. So that although a doctor may be expected in one sense always to know *when* a given technique is to be applied, yet this is still only a technical 'when'. Faced with a *given man*, a doctor might indeed deliberate whether to heal: he might decide it was better to let the man die or he might decide to back out altogether. *What to do about this man* is not a technical question unless I have already made up my mind what my aim is.[1] An answer could come from technical skill or ignorance, or from quite other considerations. And it is a mistake to avoid this, as Aristotle sometimes does, by saying that the function of a lyre-player is to play the lyre; and of a good

[1] Kant: *Fundamental Principles of the Metaphysic of Ethics*, p. 38. In the *Critique of Practical Reason* Kant decides that the so-called hypothetical imperatives are really technical principles showing how certain states of affairs may be brought about by human action. We use such theoretical knowledge in tackling practical problems: but the technical principles do not themselves determine the will. (Abbott's translation, p. 113.) See also Betty Powell, *Knowledge of Actions*, 1967, p. 38 etc., who quotes this passage. See also B. J. Diggs, 'A technical ought', *Mind*, 1960.

lyre-player to play it well. All these eponymous heroes (lyre-players, sculptors, bridle-makers, doctors and bellows-menders) are question-begging. They do not beg all the questions, but some of the more important and difficult ones. That a man is a lyre-player still leaves it open to him not to play the lyre: and to have quite other ideas as to where his good lies.[1]

There is then no code which settles practical questions about my happiness or other people's; no code which settles all the practical questions which face a man who has chosen (or has been obliged) to become a doctor. Is there any code which settles for everyone what ought to be done in any situation where one or more of the possible actions may be required by, or contrary to, morality? Kant held that there are in fact laws of duty and that these are present in the sound natural understanding of men— although he admits that 'these laws require a judgement sharpened by experience' to determine in what cases they are applicable.[2]

This last remark is clearly not a big enough concession. It may be very difficult indeed to determine whether a certain course of action would have some element of fraud in it. There is always the difficulty of having to rely on a restricted view of the facts of the case. And of course we sometimes find that the same action is both required by one duty and forbidden by another. As Mill said, it is not a blemish in a moral system that it gives rise to

[1] *Nicomachean Ethics*, Book I, Chapter 7. The doctor (above) is in Book III, Chapter 3.
[2] Kant: *Fundamental Principles of the Metaphysic of Ethics*, p. 5.

conflicting duties: all moral systems do so and this arises inevitably from 'the complicated nature of human affairs'.[1] In other words, in practical situations, our moral notions as well as our notions of happiness, are complex and unsure, and the knowledge of a set of general rules is never *all* we need to answer practical moral questions.

We have to rely on *our own view* of the facts of the case. A man might have a perfectly reliable theory about stresses and strains but yet make disastrous mistakes by wrongly identifying his materials. So also a man might have a wholly enlightened conscience but make mistakes because he misunderstands the situation he is in. It is one thing to know that you ought to relieve someone's distress: another thing to know what distress this man suffers from and how to remedy it. This is a characteristic of all practical decisions: the 'diagnosis' is based on my view of the facts: that the suggested remedy is a remedy, is a statement of fact for which there may be much or little evidence.

Theoretical questions also are settled by our applying rules to cases—by our own view of each particular case. In pure mathematics we can go wrong in such applications either by ignorance of the rules or by a simple slip in applying rules we know. In questions of the physical sciences and in historical questions, other possibilities of error are added to those found in pure mathematics. But these are also still theoretical questions. Any mistake may always be discovered later and the necessary corrections made.

[1] *Utilitarianism*, Chapter 2.

What finally distinguishes practical questions from theoretical, is that they must lead within a limited time to *action*; hence there is not unlimited time in which to make our examination: and there may or may not be an opportunity of correcting a mistake. In discussing a question in physics or history, we can normally start again from the beginning. In practical questions there is a sense in which this is never true. If the doctor changes the treatment, he has to apply the new treatment to the patient who has already suffered the old. This may be unimportant. It is often all-important.

There is a further complication. In considering a practical question we have to decide *when* to act. At any given moment only so much evidence has been collected: only certain inferences have been drawn. Am I prepared to act on these factual beliefs or not? How much evidence is good evidence in this case? Here it is easy to see that two people might agree on their view of the facts and probabilities of the case: one may be willing to act and another not. It is not the case that one is better at observation or rational inference: both agree. Here an element of personal character enters and may be decisive. One is for action now: the other is not prepared to act. But the one who declines as well as the one who takes a chance is making a decision on a practical question and will feel responsible for the outcome: and perhaps have no opportunity to act later. In practice, then, we do not choose our questions: and there is always a time-limit for the answers. We can tackle them only by reflection and observation—which are rational enough: but we have to act before we have had time to collect all the relevant evidence or perhaps even to examine what we have. And this in theoretical enquiries is simply *absurd*. But if in practical matters we try to be too rational we find ourselves spending so long over our deliberations that we are properly judged unreasonable. There is, then, a notion of what is reasonable in action and this does not normally mean simply the same as rational. It is not reasonable to be too rational. Drowning men are not necessarily unreasonable when they cling to straws.

Reasonable choice starts with rational consideration but neither in theory nor in practice do we choose our view of the facts of the case. To decide here means to consider what is *given*, and the inferences to which it leads. In every practical decision we affirm a view of the facts of the case by the way we apply our principles to a case. 'Affirm' here is equivalent with 'tacitly assert'. This affirmation may be made in great doubt but it involves coming down for one view or the other: and declining to act is coming down against the views upon which one might act and this also is an affirmation. It is then a legitimate ground of objection or criticism of what was done, that it rested upon a *false* view of the case. For example, if I forgive somebody for doing me an injury, it is a logical objection that after all he did not commit any injury. While we do not say that the action was false (which is meaningless) we say it was mistaken.

In dealing with a practical problem we apply principles of conduct: and it is sometimes said that an answer to a practical question *affirms* these principles (as it clearly affirms a view of the facts) and is open to logical objection if it can be shown that these principles are *false*. We still should not say that the *action* was false, but that it was mistaken. Other philosophers hold that the sense in which we affirm a principle of conduct is quite different from the sense in which we affirm a view of the facts: and that while an explicit statement expressing the view of the facts would simply be a true or false statement, an affirmation of a principle of conduct cannot be called either true or false in the same sense—which is the usual sense of the words. It is not a tacit *assertion*.

The second view would reject altogether the notion of true or false principles of conduct: so that if I cannot know a proposition unless that proposition is true, then I cannot be said to *know* the difference between the right and the wrong way to act. What then does an affirmation amount to, if it is not a claim to know? A claim to believe will not do, because to believe a proposition means the same as to believe that it is true. The answer which these philosophers give is that in affirming a principle of conduct I am announcing that I choose it or have chosen it: or have accepted it or do now accept it. This implies that while we do not choose our view of the facts of the case we do *choose* the principle of conduct which we apply or by which we are guided.[1]

I am inclined to say that I often take practical decisions very largely from inclination, choice, preference, liking,

---

[1] The prescriptivist theory of ethical judgements: see especially R. M. Hare, *The Language of Morals*, 1952, and *Freedom and Reason*, 1963.

disliking: and that *so far as I do so* I make a decision without affirming any general principle of conduct at all. I do not have to claim that what I like is likable: that the proposition 'X is likable' is a truth I happen to know even if others do not. Such decisions rest of course upon a view of the facts of the case which we do not choose: beyond that it rests upon a choice of mine for which I need give no reasons. That is to say I choose it without claiming that my choice can be supported by any principle of conduct. And in reaching a decision I am choosing: and until I have chosen, it is not possible for me or anyone else to know what I really want because in this matter I do not at that stage really want anything.

But where practical questions are decided upon principle, we do defend and explain a decision by reference to general maxims. So also I sometimes consider whether what is proposed to me, or what I want to do, or what I believe to be in my own best interest, is fair to others, or keeps faith or is honest: or is harsh, unjust, deceitful, wrong. I have said that these moral concepts are vague and fluctuating: that if we think of simple rules defining honesty they will need amplification and perhaps modification when we are faced with practical problems. The question now is whether in making a decision upon principle I can be said to affirm a moral principle: and if so whether this is really something that I will or adopt or accept rather than assert.

Certainly what a man does can be open to objection not on the grounds that it is irrelevant to the actual situation but that it is contrary to a principle of conduct. To flog a dead horse is pointless: to flog a living one may be objected to as cruel even if it is not pointless. To forgive an innocent man is absurd: not to forgive an enemy may be objected to as harsh and inhuman. But (granted that the anti-flogger is affirming a principle) are we obliged to say that the flogger affirms the principle that it is right to flog: does he deny that it is cruel? Does the unforgiving man affirm that we have no duty to forgive?

The opinion of Socrates is that a man cannot sincerely, and with all his wits about him, say that we have a duty to forgive and yet not himself forgive. Hence in not for-giving he is evincing his real conviction which is that we have not, in such circumstances as these, a duty to forgive.[1]

I hold that people do have convictions on practical matters and sometimes act contrary to them: that this can sometimes be discovered by interrogation of a certain form. We ask what *reason* a man had for what he did and what *reason* if any he set aside. And there are cases where a man will offer a certain kind of reason for what he did and a very different kind of reason which was a reason for not doing it and which he set aside or (as he admits) would have set aside had it occurred to him. For example men sometimes fail in professional duties: their reason for omitting the duty is something entirely non-professional which moved them more strongly than any consideration of what was required by their profession. 'I did not go out because my wife was ill and unwilling to be left alone.' And is that what is expected of a doctor? No, it is

[1] See also Chapter 3, pp. 61–2.

not. So also a man will say he told a lie to save his reputation. And is that a decent way to behave? No, it is not. His reasons for the lie are not moral: but this does not entail that he was indifferent or forgetful of the moral reasons against lying. (And we recognise also the quite different case where a man feels there are moral reasons for telling a lie here although he remains fully aware that in general lying is wrong. It may well be that in this case he *is* acting in accordance with his real moral convictions.) That one has a reason for omitting what is generally accepted as a duty does not imply that one has *moral* reasons for omitting it. On my view it may be true that a man believes lying to be wrong and yet is found telling a lie which he knows to be a lie. And it leaves it open to say that such a belief may be true or false. This it does because it does not explain that what it means to 'hold' a moral principle is *simply* to act on it when this is possible. I have offered no account of what it is to hold or tacitly affirm a moral principle. It could be that this is to be explained in just the same way as holding a factual belief: but it is also possible that to believe a moral principle is not at all the same sort of thing as to believe a factual proposition: and even that to hold a moral principle is not to claim that it is *true*. But in my view it cannot properly be called a matter of choice.

One thing is already clear: I can hold to my point of view on a moral question even if nobody else accepts it: and I cannot do this in mathematics and I cannot do it in the case of any factual science. In the second case we know that differences of opinion often occur and may be unresolvable for long enough. But this does not alter the fact that we look for agreement: and that it needs explaining if there is no agreement. The concurrence of others is one of my *criteria* for accepting or not accepting a principle of mathematics, history or science. It seems to me that it is not a criterion in the case of moral principles. But where agreement is a criterion what it leads to is my being convinced. This of course is the point of having criteria: if they are satisfied I am so far convinced. But we do also say that what we feel about our moral principles is conviction. Philosophers sometimes try to make a big distinction here: one can be driven to a conclusion in mathematics: one can be obliged to accept the evidence in history: but one cannot be driven or obliged to accept any moral point of view. I should rather say that in each case we have a kind of autonomy. I have to be convinced by the reasoning in mathematics: I have to be convinced by the evidence in science or history. This is quite different from giving up or pretending to believe. I think this is the same in morality: except that (1) our factual beliefs do not decide the issue alone and (2) there are special temptations to pretend to accept a moral principle, whether from hypocrisy, fear, ambition or fraud.

In the case of mathematics and the sciences we do not acknowledge the existence of personal criteria and we expect our common criteria to reach decisive results in (at least most branches of) mathematics: and to lead towards an accepted solution in science and history. Anyone who uses other tests is not regarded as a mathematician, scientist, historian. In moral questions we acknowledge alternative criteria and accept the fact that particular questions will be answered differently by different thinkers—all of whom may be fully conscientious. Of course if moral principles were deducible from the facts they would (like the facts) have to be decided on the criteria that are commonly accepted: and anyone who refused to accept these tests, or who introduced other tests, could be logically faulted. This does not seem to me to be the case in moral disagreements. But there are here limits as to what we accept as moral criteria. I should agree with Bentham that they must have a bearing on human happiness and suffering, or at the least on the fulfilment or denial of human aims. (This view has been supported in recent years by Philippa Foot's interesting paradoxes.[1]) It follows that it is possible for two people, considering the same question and agreeing on their view of the facts and probabilities of the case, to disagree on what it is right to do. This will happen where they employ different tests of what is good and bad for men, have different scales for what is kind or harsh, different notions of what is cruel. Conversely, it is possible (it may happen) that two people considering the same question from precisely the same moral point of view will give different answers. This may happen where they find themselves in disagreement over the facts of the case.

What I have now to do is to show that What is the Meaning of Life? is itself a practical problem: and that if

[1] Philippa Foot: 'When is a principle a moral principle?' Aristotelian Society. Supp. Vol. 28, 1954.

we think we have an *answer* to the question, then that answer (1) asserts a view about the facts; (2) affirms some principles of conduct. (1) Such an answer then can be logically criticised: it can be shown that the view of the facts is false or that there are not sufficient grounds for accepting it. (2) It can also be said that in determining what is the Meaning of Life one must be guided by some principles of choice, some convictions about what is good or rewarding: and one could be criticised on the grounds that these are mistaken principles. Of course criticism may and normally does combine comment of both kinds.

There is a peculiar difficulty about knowing the facts: it is peculiar not just to this question of the meaning of life but to all practical questions. In asking the facts about life we find ourselves asking about what man can do as well as what man has done or is doing.[1] And the truth or falsity of assertions about what man can do depends in part on man's own will and efforts: on his courage, perseverance, loyalty, stability. (As in any practical question one finds oneself asking: Can I hold on? Can I hold out?) Here we are often called upon to make an effort to make our beliefs come true. This is quite different from the effort which a scientist or historian is called upon to make. He tries (from time to time—he has all the time there is and if he dies too soon there are others to take the matter further) to *test* the truth of his belief, to discover whether it is true or false: not to make it come true. Indeed the real point of the effort is often to try to show that the belief is false—is inconsistent with the

[1] See also Chapter 6, pp. 144–5.

evidence. In tackling the question of the Meaning of Life one may well form a view as to what man can do and set out to make that belief 'come true'. And there is not the slightest whiff of intellectual duplicity in it. It implies that we are committing ourselves to doubtful propositions. But to feel obliged to commit oneself to doubtful propositions is of the very essence of practical questions.

CHAPTER 8

TAKING THINGS AS THEY ARE

◇◇◇

THERE ARE certain general truths about ourselves and the world which we have to acknowledge. Many views as to what the meaning of life is are refuted simply enough by showing that they rest upon a false opinion about what we are. This is true of many authoritative and many popular answers to the question. On examination they are shown to rest on a one-sided incomplete view of man—whether romantic or censorious. There are, for example, all those views which incorporate the belief that man is capable of achieving all the time anything he is capable of achieving sometimes. There are those views which represent the self as an enemy to be suppressed or an impediment to be abandoned in favour of something else. There are views which require us always to subordinate the present to the future. Where do people get such ideas? Certainly not from a dispassionate consideration of the kind of creature man is. To find (not invent) the meaning of life, if it has a meaning, it is necessary to consider the Facts of Life: and this means its contingent limitations and opportunities. In the first part of this chapter I shall be concerned with the contingent limitations. The question of the necessary limitations (i.e. the logically necessary ones) will not here present difficulties. The question of what is *in fact* a limitation—what we had better accept as an unavoidable although contingent limitation—is sometimes difficult. It may involve an element of judgement. Questions of what is negligence in law, what is unnecessary suffering in morals, involve judgement in this way. But while these are questions relating to certain given circumstances, we are concerned with a logically prior question: what in general is *given*, what are in general the contingent limitations of life.

How, exactly, is man limited? Philosophers have dwelt on certain 'necessary truths' which hold in the world, as though these were the important factors that limit our lives and set our course. But if they are necessary they must limit any being, including God. If so they cannot really count as restrictions on what can be actual but as the limitations of what is logically possible. What we mean by 'logically possible' is defined by necessary truths. They *constitute* the possible and do not in themselves determine what possibilities are to be actualised.

These so-called limitations appear to us as wholly rational, wholly intelligible. The real limitations spring from what in the past has been called contingency. That a given man exists is a contingent fact: all existential propositions about finite beings are contingent. Contingency constitutes man and limits his activities and choices.

These limitations may be distinguished into three groups. (1) There are hard facts about me that I can imagine otherwise. I might have been taller or shorter, stronger or more strong-willed than I am: I might have been a novelist or a farmer. (2) It is possible to speak of great changes in human life. We might have been the largest of all living creatures: we might all of us have been tremendously far-sighted or gifted with far more delicate sensibilities: we might have been even more insensible to each other than we are. All this is vaguely imaginable and we may feel glad or sorry that we are not like this. Further differences (still not nonsense) are perhaps not very fully imaginable: we might have been totally incapable of pain or pleasure: we might have been omniscient, indestructible, immutable, perhaps incorporeal. (3) It is a fact, a contingency, that we live in a common world at all. It is logically possible for us to describe what we see in any set of categories: but all the same it is a fact that only certain categories are used. There are terms on whose use we can all agree. It is conceivable that we might not have been able to recognise the shapes and colours and sounds we all do recognise; or to count or measure things in such a way as to agree in our findings. That we do agree up to a point is a matter of fact. But it is this fact that gives our language its shape: and in particular it enables us to agree about what belongs to the common world and what to one's own inner life.

I shall take these contingencies in the reverse order and begin with these most fundamental facts about our common language. It is here that it is important not to confuse necessary analytical truths with contingent truths.

For example we can think of the rules of simple arithmetic (addition, multiplication) as logical deductions or elaborations of conventionally established axioms. They are necessary but vacuous. 'A proposition of mathematics does not express a thought.'[1] But the terms defined in arithmetic are called 'numbers' because we use them in describing actual observed things. The whole *point* of necessary truths is that they define concepts which occur in contingent truths: 'Here are five cows: here are seven more: so there are now twelve cows.'

We cannot say that the truths of arithmetic apply to our world *necessarily*. And yet if in fact they did not apply as they do, the objects would have to be extraordinarily different, or we should.

Two situations seem distinguishable. (1) I have made up a calculus, a language, a code, and it never tells me anything new because the only formulae I can construct are determined by the rules I made. (2) I am confronted by objects in whose construction I had no part: I observe and enumerate them and I describe them and record their changes. What I am now suggesting is that we cannot really hold these two apart. I use *a language* (a particular system of signs) in order to describe what I observe: from these records I make all sorts of logical and mathematical deductions and am confident that the inferred propositions (which are *about* the things I observed) will be shown by fresh observations to be true: and of course by anybody's observations. One might explain this by saying: if there is a discrepancy I deal with it by doubting one or other of my observations or by doubting my calculation;

[1] Wittgenstein: *Tractatus Logico-Philosophicus*, 6.21.

and in one way or the other *I can always secure agreement*. This is true: but sounds outrageously unfair to us all. We do not abandon our experimental results in order to fit in with the results calculated—unless there is empirical evidence that the results were mistakenly collected or recorded. And certainly the last thing we should do would be to 'correct' our calculations in order to fit the independently observed 'verification': that is, unless we identify an actual mistake in our calculations. The fact is that we do not have to resort to subterfuges in order to find agreement. We can and do work together in the most high-principled fashion. How is this possible? Our world permits it. Our use of a calculus and of descriptive terms implies that we *can* agree in our use. We in our world are capable of it. There is a common world of objects. And its limitations at this level mark the shape of our inner worlds.[1]

What we see or hear belongs to the public world: but *that* I see and hear is a fact of my private world. *I cannot confuse my own seeing or my own remembering with anybody else's.* And here again we build up a system of necessary or linguistic truths upon a basis of fact. The difference between what I see or remember and my seeing or remembering is shown in what it makes sense to say of the one and not of the other: but it rests on a difference about the way things *are*. People generally confirm what I see and (with less regularity) what I remember. I do not ask anyone to confirm *that* I see or *that* I remember; or

[1] Wittgenstein: *Philosophical Investigations*, Part I, §§241–2.

176

that I hope or dread or like or dislike. If they did, if I could expect them to do so, the whole grammar of our language would need to be changed. The notion of 'person' would be lost.

Of course we can up to a point imagine that these things were not possible to us. The other animals do not tell each other about what they see, how things seem or feel to them. But neither do they talk about what things there are. However, our ability to talk to each other clearly connects with an ability which animals share: for they, like us, can perceive the world and deal with it. What I think verges on the unintelligible is that there should be people who share a language in which to talk about things in the world but have no language at all in which to talk of their inner life. If they were unaware of each other as having an inner life they would, of course, be unaware of the existence of other *persons*. Then perhaps they do not notice their fellow-beings in pleasure or pain or purposive activity—are blankly unaware of it. How could this be? Because nobody gives any sign that he is in pain or happy or frightened? That is to say, the behaviour we so quickly notice in animals is absent in men? Or perhaps they observe it but feel nothing and so take no account of it? Unlike all the higher animals.

It is a fact that we can interpret the behaviour of men and animals in such a way as to describe in a common language what goes on in our inner life. The conclusion of all this is that to come to terms with life we have to come to terms with ourselves and with the world outside us. And the world outside us is a common world, shared with others: against the background of which we not only make the distinction (of immense practical importance) between ourselves and the world: we are also able to some extent to share our private world with others and to share in their private world. To see the same things is a way of sharing: but so also is to feel the same fear: although there are here logical differences in the use of the word 'same'.

We did not choose to be born and we did not choose our country or the times in which we find ourselves. Whether it makes sense to speak of my exercising a choice in such matters is a very difficult question, but certainly I did not exercise any such choice. So also we did not choose our parents and they did not choose us:

> O little did my Mither ken
> The day she cradled me
> The lands I was to travel in
> Or the death I was to dee.

Perhaps she did indeed wonder: but she could not choose for us.

Even this hardly goes to the bottom of it all. We did not choose our bodies: and just as men may be passionately attached to their country, parents, language, children, without having ever *selected* them, so I believe men are in general passionately attached to the shape of the human body. We find it very hard to imagine people in other shapes and are resentful of any gross misrepresentation of the human body.

I believe that our feeling for life, our whole attitude

towards our fellow-creatures, is conditioned by these great 'Facts of Life'. We know what it is to be virtuous or vicious—to act well or badly—in a world in which people are born; enjoy and suffer; are in love or out of love; and in which all grow old and die. We may try to imagine a life in which there is no pain or suffering: even a world in which there is no death. Can we form any clear picture of it? Can we work it out? As Hume remarks, many people profess to believe that we shall one day perhaps belong to such a world: but the belief is so alien to our whole way of thinking and feeling that it affects us very little, perhaps not at all.[1] I should go so far as to ask: Is it all *really* imaginable? Can it be thought out fully? What sort of beings would these be and what sort of life and institutions would they have? What sort of aims or ends? I think we simply do not know what to feel about them: they do not come alive for us. Are such possibilities in any way relevant to our lives? That they can be made entertaining I allow: but to be entertaining they do not even have to be logically coherent. Can we form a clear picture of a world in which people do not grow old? One of the great merits of Bishop Butler's *Sermons* is that he there views the moral life concretely, as the life of creatures placed as we are placed in this world. For example, in his sermon on 'The Forgiveness of Injuries' he argues that if you postpone a reconciliation with your enemy he may die before you have forgiven

[1] Hume: *Treatise of Human Nature*, Book I, Part iii, §9. Butler: *Sermons*, IX, at the end. See also Keats: 'He has his winter too of pale misfeature, Or else he would forego his mortal nature.'

him: and then, Butler asks, How will you feel about this when your turn comes and you are going to die? This is indeed an *argumentum ad hominem*: it cuts no ice with the angels.

That we must make decisions on incomplete evidence —this is surely one of the absolutely fundamental facts about our life: a fact upon which our only notion of reasonable conduct depends. Can we really imagine a world in which we could *know* the consequences of our actions and our choices? Our notion of what is virtuous and what is vicious presupposes that we have to choose without being able to foretell the consequences of our decisions. Of course we can make an estimate: this is what we all must do because we feel responsible for what we do. But we must act

> —this way or that—
> 'Tis done, and in the after-vacancy
> We wonder at ourselves like men betrayed.[1]

Although we cannot control the outcome of our choices, even so we feel responsible for doing the best we can with what we have while we have it.

And in each life there are particular choices. Things loom very large in our lives which we did indeed choose, but on very insufficient evidence. We have to have a job. Perhaps we consider carefully what would suit us best. But we cannot go on deliberating about this problem indefinitely: so at some point, and on very incomplete evidence, we make a choice.

[1] Wordsworth: *The Borderers*, Act III, l. 1540,

Much the same is true of marriage. A man *might* set about this task in a rational calculating fashion: but he would only get himself laughed at if he did. Rational? Perhaps: but most unreasonable. David Hume, in a letter about his brother's marriage, remarked that wives 'are the only heavenly bodies whose orbits are as yet uncertain'.[1] If a man is so *rational* that he cannot decide whom to marry without a full consideration of the statistical evidence—then he will never leave a legitimate heir. So that, as we say, 'marriages are made in Heaven'. And many of those who do not marry do not choose, or only half-choose, not to marry.

Do we really choose our friends? Only in part. Did we choose the moral code under which we live? No: but of course we are free to modify it. Did we choose our religion? Very few of us did: and today the big majority of people who (without giving up religion altogether) change from one religion or one church to another, do so on account of marriage. And by most people this is accepted as a perfectly proper step to take: and I believe this is a most revealing fact about religion. Here are two factors—marriage and religion—of immense importance in our inner life: if at all possible, they must not be permitted to conflict. That is reasonable enough and generally accepted as reasonable. But whether one could call it *rational* is quite another matter. How can it be rational? And this illustrates as well as anything can, what I mean by saying that our lives are *limited*.[2]

[1] See E. C. Mossner: *Life of David Hume*, p. 240.
[2] I am not of course condoning any attempts by authorities to impose conditions upon 'mixed marriages'.

These choices matter to me: and to choose is to be guided by some general considerations. It seems to be a necessary condition for life to have a meaning, that I should be capable of being guided by my own convictions. These may be intuitive: they may be reached only after long analysis and reflection. The thinking may not be at all original in the sense of novel: but it must be original in the sense that I am led by my own reflections to my own decision. I may of course consider what I am recommended to believe or commanded to believe: I may decide to follow the example of somebody without asking how he reaches his decisions. These are all included in 'my own convictions' and 'thinking things out for myself'. Unless I do this, can my life have meaning? We have in fact opportunities for making decisions: and I cannot see how life could have meaning unless we were capable of making our own decisions and being guided by them.

But to be guided by general considerations is to appeal to common standards. Life could have no meaning if I could never *identify* a mistake. Speech is meaningless if there is no way of showing when it is correctly used and when not. So that to reject the whole enterprise of having rules in common with others, and applying them to the best of our ability—to reject all this would be to deprive life of all meaning. It is to isolate oneself: to pose as the only person or the only non-person. To this plight a man may be driven by extreme fear or pain or confusion: and in this state life for him is without meaning.

What other conditions must hold if life is to have meaning?

Secondly, that my own life matters. What I do, enjoy, and suffer: including the enjoyment of the world, the pursuit of the intellect and the arts for their own sake. I should say a man's life matters *because it does or might matter to him*. Rocks and stones and trees matter if they matter to somebody. A person inevitably matters just because he matters or might matter to himself. If this were not so, life would have no meaning. There are people who sometimes cannot care at all about their own life and cannot believe that it has any meaning. It may be in some cases that they are asking the wrong question. *Does my life matter?* This could be taken to mean: Has it any importance in the world at all? What sense of *importance* is in question? One might argue that the only proper way to estimate importance is by reference to the public world. Then it matters that a great many people are often in pain because this leads to a National Health Service; it matters that a lot of people fall in love because this leads to a large increase of the population; it matters that most people are afraid of suffering because this leads them to obey the law and behave in a regular and pre-dictable manner. It matters that we all die because if we did not where should we all live?

Of course all this is true in what it asserts. And I suppose the logical conclusion is that people's lives matter in the mass: but the birth or death, or suffering or rapture, of this or that man, matters very little if at all.

However, it does seem to be generally admitted that my birth and death matter *to me*. No doubt the world would not have been very different if I had never been born or if I had died in infancy. But (one wants to say, if this is not nonsense), it would have made a lot of difference to me—a world of difference. And it must have made all the difference to my children too. No doubt the world was not very different before I was born: but to ask 'How would the world be different if I died now?' is (or may be) to ask a curious question. It is not at all like asking 'How would the world be different if this or that physical object were to disappear?' When I die *something* will go out of the world that nothing can replace. So that I do matter to myself: or if in fact I do not, yet I might matter to myself. Clearly without this condition life could have no meaning.

The third consideration is that people matter or may matter to each other. This concern for others may be positive or negative: when we look for the meaning of our lives we look not only within but also to other people. Even the most solitary or self-sufficient, the most lonely or disillusioned, will not deny that the question of the meaning of life turns in part on his relationships to other people. Our concern for other people is not simply to make use of them or to be of use to them. We regard relationships with other people as good or bad in themselves.

It is tempting to say that life has meaning where there are positive relationships (such as affection or admiration) and these are reciprocated. But some human relationships cannot be reciprocal—that of parent to child and its converse. All the more important lasting relationships between people are many-stranded and some elements may be reciprocal, some complementary, others not.

We may have admiration on one side and amusement on the other. It is surely pedantic and absurd to insist on particular patterns.

Hatred, envy, malice, despair are also not indifference: they belong to the facts of life. I do not myself find it easy to imagine life without them. They are there: they may be condemned, avoided where possible; they may or may not have a place in the pattern of life a man attempts to follow.

One of the great 'injustices' of life is that some people fail to achieve the most important mutual relationships. Their lives still matter: it is an essential condition of such relationships between people that each person's own life matters. Nevertheless the possibility of positive mutual concern seems to me fundamental. It is a fact of life that all the higher animals enjoy each other's society in one direction or another: the existence of life in mammalian species depends upon it; in human society the existence of speech depends on it. In man the relationship is apprehended and valued for itself. It is a fact that a meal unshared loses much of its value—not all. The frustration of the solitary may lead him or her to deny that life has any meaning. Against this one can only argue that the possibility of a positive relationship remains even if the hope of it has vanished: and that there is still something logically prior—the concern a man has or may have for his own life.

A fourth consideration is that in an individual life there is the possibility of a particular pattern. Things that we choose and do, things that we do not choose, but which happen, may add up to something. I believe people commonly think that it is entirely up to them to choose a pattern and impose it on their lives. A 'career' is thought of as such a pattern even though success is seen to be partly a matter of chance: i.e. success comes partly by the agent's own planning, partly by his cleverness in making the best of his chances—hence at last, partly by chance. At all events, the pattern is thought of as something one can in the main 'take credit for'. My main argument in this chapter is that our lives are shaped very largely by good and bad chances—by things we did not plan or foresee or perhaps understand. And when I say that there is the possibility of a pattern in an individual life, I mean to include these unchosen elements—what is given. Where such a pattern is accepted it can serve as a guide: and adds to 'the meaning of my life'.

This kind of pattern logically presupposes that a man matters to himself and that people matter to each other. But we can imagine a life without a pattern: and most of us have experienced stages in which life had no pattern: and stages in which some configuration breaks up and life begins to wear a different look.

I represent it as a matter of fact about life that we can look for a particular pattern and go on looking until we find a pattern we can accept. An accepted pattern is of immense practical importance. Up to a point it answers the question: 'How am I to live? What am I to do with my life?'[1]

[1] 'Adding up to something': John Wisdom: *Philosophy and Psycho-Analysis*, p. 153—a quotation from J. P. Marquand.

Both 'looking for a pattern' and 'accepting a pattern' are to be understood in a certain way. By the first I exclude the notion of 'total choice': I introduce the notion of accepting certain things in life as *given*. But of course many given situations call for choice, even if very limited choice. I have tried to give my own view that life involves doing as well as understanding. To detect a pattern has an element of quietism in it: certainly it is anti-idealistic. I hope to find a shape to life that I can adopt, that I can identify myself with. But it is not one I shall take full credit for. In accepting the pattern I do not condemn all other patterns: I do not pretend that no better pattern can be conceived. I make the practical decision that this is *sufficient for me*.

I am speaking of the possibility that an individual life may have its own pattern. But in accepting we must be applying some general principles of evaluation. We expect others to share such principles: but not that they should or could be led to accept for themselves the same pattern. Because the individual pattern includes elements that are given, not chosen: and because two people who both value the same thing, are likely to give it a different place in their lives.

And when I speak of 'accepting a pattern', I do not mean that, having a pattern, *everything* I do will be governed by it. This could not be so because the pattern includes 'given' elements which I did not choose and which may themselves change without my wishing it. For example I shall grow older and this will in time en-large or restrict my choices: I have now relationships

7   BPA

with other people and they may die or depart or may themselves withdraw from my society. As life goes on, having a pattern in no way makes me immune from the unexpected fortunes and misfortunes of life.

But I should add as a second most important principle: by 'accepting a pattern' I do not mean making all one's choices by it. What is important for life to have a meaning is that there can be an acceptable pattern in an individual's life: not that there must be this or that particular pattern. A man who has a closed set of principles by which he must judge every public situation is called doctrinaire. And I think we all recognise that some people attempt to settle all choices in their private lives by a single idea of themselves. In a very special sense one might call them romantics: and they are distinguished as *taking themselves too seriously*. Perhaps this is a misdescription: they take their single idea of themselves too seriously and their actual and potential selves not seriously enough. It is true of many people that besides the pattern their life shows they have other ideas of themselves. They often retreat into them and spend many 'idle' hours embellishing them. Such a pattern may be highly fantastic: or it may simply be 'the road not taken': the other self a man could not actually *be*. At all events, whatever pattern of life a man may accept for himself, it seems that it is also necessary to allow oneself time out. Unless a man allows himself this disengagement he will not have a mind free and open to many things which simply happen to him, which he might enjoy, but which could not have been found by following a pattern. Here again, since the original pattern depends to a great extent upon un-planned circumstances, following a pattern in this sense of the word 'pattern' must allow for such openness and freedom, and even disengagement.

A man may accept a pattern without a great deal of deliberate and self-conscious analysis. The amount of rational reflexion involved depends upon the character and intellect of the person concerned. These general reflexions on the matter are intended for reflective readers. Mill and Butler, both deeply reflective by character and profession, warn us against too strict adherence to calculation, analysis, idealisation.[1]

My conclusion is that life *has* meaning because of the following facts—if they are facts but not if they are inventions:

(1) A man may be guided by his own convictions.

(2) The life of a person matters in itself: because it may matter to him and it may matter to other people.

(3) The relationships between persons matter in them-selves and many are of value in themselves.

(4) A person may detect and accept a particular pattern in his own life. If so, he may be guided by it in the restricted sense I have explained.

These conclusions may seem disappointing because they indicate only possibilities: and the second has an element of maybe in it: for a man *may say* that nothing in his own life matters to him and cease to exercise any

---

[1] Butler: *Sermons*, XI is near the point; Mill: *Autobiography*, Chapter V is absolutely on this point.

rational choice. If this verdict is not a misapprehension (as I feel sure it very often is) then here again the fact is that a man's life *may* matter to him.

The conclusions look thin partly because they are so general: (4) is of course deliberately permissive, pluralistic —declines to outline a single pattern for all lives: and declines to fasten a single pattern over the whole of a single life. If they *are* thin, I cannot apologise: I am trying to find things, not invent them.

The objection can also be made that 'the meaning of life' refers to the meaning of the whole, not only to the lives of persons. And I have already admitted that those who ask whether there *is* any meaning at all, are asking whether there is something *in the world at large* which sets us to fulfil some particular pattern or pursue some particular goal.

My answer is (1) that for life to have a meaning there must be a boundary between me and the world; and (2) we can know that the world is such as to permit the existence of persons of whom my very narrow statements hold good. It permits some to reach supreme excellence in life and in art. So far as we know it also permits the defeat and destruction of any aim anyone ever set himself.

A man may say: I cannot be satisfied with these mere possibilities: there is no sense in life unless there is *some* ground for believing that the world or God is on the side of those things which matter to us: the good of the soul, the communion of the virtuous. But if there were ground for believing this, should we not have to admit that we might be mistaken in identifying the things that matter to God, the kinds of life that are really virtuous? To this the reply will be a further demand: we must have some assurance that we can know what is good—not inerrably but with a chance of correcting our mistakes in the long run.

CHAPTER 9

RELIGION AND THE MEANING
OF LIFE

◇◇

I HAVE ARGUED that life has a meaning and that this arises from the possibilities which remain in the face of all actualities. I am not merely saying that the lives of some people have meaning: I am saying that the life of any man does have meaning.

It may be objected: These possibilities are not enough: there can be no sense in life unless there is some ground for believing that a man's life has some particular place in the whole: that there is in the whole a power for righteousness: and that there is some means by which we can come to know what God counts as righteousness: hence for supposing that if we see a plan in our own lives, it is God's plan. Unless we can say this, all that has been done is to show that one might find *a plan*, not *the plan*: and if we simply have *a plan*, we have absolutely no reason to expect that it is feasible, that if we try hard enough we can achieve something. We may achieve nothing: and that will not matter except to us.

Religion tries to provide two great assurances: that there is an absolute good and bad in the world at large: and that the absolute good has power. Many important consequences are derived: God's goodness is seen in his relationship to us, we matter to God, we can know that we are in his keeping in life and in death. God has *the* plan for our lives and we must (somehow) look for it and try to carry it out. In this attempt God supports us. And somehow and somewhere there is justice. God's view of our lives is the true view: his judgement is wholly just: and in the end, in some way, we can be sure that what we receive is not unjust: if it is mercy—it is not mercy at someone else's expense.

The strength of this theological position is that it turns my hypotheticals into categoricals. Some people's lives do not matter to them: I have said only that it is possible that a man's life *may* matter to him. I have also added (mysteriously) that in some sense a person does matter because he *may* matter to himself. This is readily translated into theological language: because a person is the kind of being who may matter to himself, for this very reason his life matters to God. God has (not *might have*) a concern for every man. Again evidently one man *may* matter to another: but if we are candid we have to admit that there are people for whom we have no concern—there are people we know well who seem unworthy of our concern. The theological view does not have to say they are not unworthy in themselves: they are a matter of concern to God and for that reason (very often for no other reason) they can be a matter of concern to us. Again, in detecting a pattern in his life a man may be very dubious as to whether there is any pattern or whether he has discovered the 'right' pattern. And it may seem to him not worth while to try to work out a pattern unless he has some assurance that he can succeed in the long run.

The theological view usually is that the 'right' pattern is the one shaped for us by God and the power of God is a guarantee that our efforts can at least bear some fruit. This may take a particular form: a man may feel that failure to do what he knows he ought to do will always dog his steps: and that he cannot go on and leave his failure behind without some kind of forgiveness. One might say: He knows he will do things for which he *cannot* forgive himself and this is a kind of standstill for him. Not everyone feels this: but I suspect many people feel it who do not admit it.

Certainly in particular enterprises it can be quite unreasonable to go ahead without some kind of assurance that success is possible. The desire for this kind of confidence in life is extremely familiar: and we see people who actually have it. Sometimes it is just a kind of self-confidence: sometimes it springs from religious belief. In adverse circumstances a man may lose his self-confidence and his life may lose its meaning. And a religious man who loses his faith may find that life has lost its meaning. But a religious man may find in God not only assurance of possible achievement, but also forgiveness of actual sin: the ability to go on in spite of failure.

It seems clear to me that in the sense explained, life may have a meaning for any person whether or not he has religious beliefs. In this chapter I want to consider whether there is ever any *good reason* for accepting religious beliefs: in particular where the acceptance or the holding fast to religious beliefs gives my life a meaning in a much more important sense than it could otherwise have—would this be a good reason for believing? A good reason is one I need not be ashamed to admit to myself and one which on the face of it would be expected to carry some weight with any reasonable man: although it could well be that with some its weight will be decisive, with others not decisive. This view of religious belief is Pragmatic. It takes for granted that if we consider the question of the universe from a purely theoretical point of view, we see that religious questions simply cannot be decided. A rational consideration of what we know of the world does not suffice. Pragmatism is the view that the question of belief in God is one we have to settle for ourselves within our limited lives: and that it is reasonable for us to come to a conclusion for or against on the limited evidence we have. We may make up our minds to believe or disbelieve because, where there is evidence pointing both ways, we cannot *go* both ways. Then there is a good reason to believe (in the Pragmatic view) if there is no decisive reason against, great gain if it were true, and we are prepared to risk the consequences of acting on our decision. Of course everybody is a pragmatist about many questions of belief: because everyone has to make practical decisions on inconclusive evidence. What distinguishes Pragmatism as a view about belief, is that there are certain fundamental metaphysical questions which it is proper to decide *in the same sort of way* as we decide which routes to take over flooded country, which of two guides to trust, which of two people to marry. I think a Rationalist must be one who holds that there are good rational grounds for accepting or rejecting religious belief, or one who simply postpones an answer—knowing that he will never be in a position to answer. It must then be part of the Pragmatist view that whether God exists or not is a question of practical importance. He cannot view it, as David Hume did, as a matter of no practical importance to man—a question of palaeontology.[1] It would be generally agreed that a question may have purely theoretical interest for some people but vital practical interest for others. What might well be disputed—what the Pragmatist needs to explain—is how metaphysical questions can be viewed by some as of vital practical concern; and be seen by others as of purely theoretical interest. Of course the explanation would be that the questions are understood differently by different people. (Which means that they are really asking different questions without recognising it.) I have tried to show that questions about 'Where did the Universe come from? What is it all leading to?' can be understood in different ways: as referring to Efficient Cause or to Efficient and Final Cause, for example.[2]

I have argued throughout that the question of the meaning of life is of practical importance: that it involves

[1] 'Palaeontology: the study of extinct forms of organised beings', Hume: *Dialogues concerning Natural Religion*, XII, at the end. This is Hume's conclusion concerning the only sort of religion he can countenance. In *The Natural History of Religion* he argues that religions exist to meet emotional needs: they are essentially practical and make all the difference to life. But in Hume's view no reasonable man can accept any of them.

[2] Cf. Chapter 5, pp. 109–11.

considering the evidence we have: making judgements according to our own lights as to what is and what is not good: following hints and leads in our own lives: and so deciding what is the point of life for us. If we were to do this we should have a guide: it is therefore something we need to make up our minds about while there is time to make use of it. The conclusions reached in the last chapter are metaphysical and have bearing on the way we think as well as on the way we live. They are metaphysical in the sense that they rest on taking things as they are, ourselves and the world, excluding nothing. We might say that they involve a view of the world as seen *from within*. But the question of religious belief seems to go beyond this: it seems to demand a view of the world *from without*.

Consider first the view that goodness is what God wills: the plan of each life is God's plan. What view are we to take of God's goodness? If we think of God as transcending our life altogether it would be possible that we know nothing at all of God's goodness. The puzzle then would be: How are we to learn what is goodness in God's sight? Certainly it could be the case that our notions of goodness contradict his. A kinder way of putting it is that what we mean by justice and righteousness fall far, far below God's justice and righteousness. An unkinder way of putting it is: What we call injustice, cruelty, everlasting vengeance, is what in God's eyes is good and just. If this is a possibility what are we to do about it? We could say: Then God is after all evil—or may be evil. If so, let us defy him as long as we live. This would be to cling to 'goodness' as we know it and reject that which is enthroned in the world at large. But who ever takes this view? Who ever argues that God is or may be evil, except hypothetically? (If there were a God we should be obliged to call him evil. And the conclusion regularly drawn from this, is that there is no God.) Who wants to proclaim an evil God?

Of course to try to consider God's righteousness from outside is not necessarily to conclude that it contradicts our own concept of virtue and vice. The difficulty is: How are we to know and what should we do if we *did* find it contradicted our notions? It seems to me questionable whether the true righteousness could be something altogether contrary to what we recognise as such from within. *Could* righteousness be simply what is commanded from without? Hume considers the view that virtue and vice might be distinctions which we are taught simply by our rulers. (They offer no explanations: they teach us certain actions are 'right' and certain actions 'wrong'.) Hume argues that this view of the origins of virtue and vice is incoherent: whatever distinctions we learned in this way—and of course there is no difficulty in imagining that distinctions could be learned in this way—would not be the distinction we all make between virtue and vice. (One might say *right* and *wrong* would be terms like *right* and *left*.) I think this view is correct: and the situation is not obviously different if for human rulers we substitute simply God. I think it follows that the view that there is a good God, arises from the view of goodness we get from inside, from our own life. If we say: 'But there must be justice in the world', we do not mean by 'justice' an unknown rule of an unknown God. We derive our notion of justice, and our demand for justice in the world at large, from the notions of justice we find in human life. We have absolutely no other conception of what justice is.

On this Pragmatic view God performs a logical function. Talk of God is talk of an absolute standard. It does not actually settle differences of judgement about what is fair and good: it says there is a correct view, not which view is correct. But the views in question are our views, got from inside. The reference to God is not pointless: we feel we must live our lives responsibly—as those who have to render account for what they have done. To render account to God implies that (1) we do not overlook the possibility that our notion of right and wrong may be mistaken: (2) we cannot stand corrected unless and until we in our own hearts are convinced of error: (3) we do not accept as a final judgement on our actions any outsider's view of what we did and why we did it. The appeal is to the truth of the matter, to the facts of the case. So that this appeal to God is an appeal to righteousness and justice as they really are: but not to an outside and imposed standard. The logical force is simply: Although I may be led to see I was mistaken, I have to act on my view of what is righteous—what else can I do? This is all another way of saying that a man must be led by his own convictions: he *can* be: and if he is not, life loses all meaning. And a conviction implies a standard of correct or incorrect. If we talk of God's righteousness, *this is* the standard of correct and incorrect. In practice we have to act when we are not certain—not certain of the facts and not certain which is the just action. But to decline to do this is in fact unreasonable and incoherent.

On this view it is still a puzzle what to do, how to live: and in theological terms—how to know and do God's will. But the whole point and content of 'God's will' arises from our own notion of what is right and our own attempts to pick up clues as to the pattern for our own lives. Whatever particular guidance is offered by religion—by reading the Bible for example—it remains a task for me to interpret and to identify God's will for me.

On this view again, the power of God is seen in the world from within. However one may come to believe that God's power is at work, the final proof is to be found in our own lives. Unless it is a power working for what we recognise as good, it cannot be the power of God. It is of course most important always to bear in mind that we are thinking of what is righteous and not what is to our own advantage. To ignore this is to overlook the third of the points made in Chapter 8: that life matters to others: that other people matter to me.

I have tried to explain how I understand talk about God's moral character. But it remains to be asked: What exactly is supposed to be the metaphysical status of God? Are we led to think of God by what we know of the universe at large? Are we trying to take a look at the universe 'as a whole': are we trying to step outside and look at the universe from outside?

I have already argued that an enquiry into the nature of the world becomes more and more remote from the conduct of our lives. The beliefs that (as it might be argued by a Pragmatist) we are led to accept for practical reasons, are about ourselves, our lives, our deaths. The temptation to believe arises from the view we have of our life from within: from questions and doubts which arise from taking things as they are. The answers go beyond things as they are. A man who can say: 'God will guide me', 'God will defend me', 'God will forgive me', 'God will not let me starve' is no doubt expressing attitudes: but it seems clear that he is making statements (by implication) which time will confirm or refute: and he would claim that experience supports such statements. But while experience may give a man some reason for such beliefs, they cannot give him conclusive reason. And it is generally agreed that such beliefs 'go beyond the facts' at least in the sense that (say) confidence in an acquaintance 'goes beyond the facts'. Those who are trustful are sometimes deceived. When a religious man finds that his trust in God has been misplaced he will not say: 'Well, God has his moods like the rest of us': nor will he forgive God for his lapse. He will think that the 'misplacing' is somehow his own: he has not correctly interpreted the will of God. And of course one begins to think of deceived husbands who *cannot* be convinced of their wife's infidelity: of people whose trust in others is unreasonable and absurd. So of course may a religion be.

But if some people are not disillusioned this may not always be because they do indeed have some kind of gift which prevents them from banking on God for the wrong things. (As I have said, this would not be a special *cleverness*.) They may just be fortunate: but it must not be assumed that it is characteristic of the religious man to be incapable of believing that his trust was misplaced. Because after all, do we not all know many people who have given up their religion for this very reason? Many have come to the conclusion that God does not guide them, or keep watch over them or forgive them.

It is not easy to get the emphasis right. I want to say again: These beliefs are practical: a man may cling to an opinion as a drowning man clings to a straw. Again the belief connects with one's whole attitude to life. A general must have confidence in his troops: and at the point when it ought to dwindle to vanishing point his own mad courage leads him to order them all to advance to destruction. So also a man who trusts his acquaintances too far may be too proud to change his ways. He may also reflect: I do not wish to live in any other way: if people cheat me—let them. Even here we cannot say that nothing will alter his stance: of course it may. But his idea of his own life keeps him on a path which other people regard as ridiculous. Should one too easily conclude that *for him* it is unreasonable?

This is the mêlée of life: and here it is that religion is best observed. And certainly some of the important religious beliefs seem more a matter of declaring an attitude than asserting a fact. If 'God will defend me' has factual implications, what of 'I am forgiven'? This means: I can go on: but it will be supported by reasons which make it like the statement 'She has forgiven me', which is certainly factual.

I want to present the statements of belief and the statements of attitude alongside each other: and to say that if
this makes religion seem a great muddle, *so are all our
practical affairs*. If religion seems even more muddled,
surely the explanation chiefly lies in the fact that the needs
which men try to meet by their religion are needs of
which they are not fully conscious: needs which have
their first beginnings in childhood. They do not disappear as we grow up because in growing up we are not
altogether cut off from our childhood. And nobody has
yet shown that we should still be truly human beings if
we were.[1]

The childishness appears in myth. And of course the
language of myths is often (especially in sophisticated
religions) transcendental. The myth appears to take an
outside look at the whole: to oppose to the world we
know another world, an infinite being. This can be said
to show that our lives are limited. Our world (the world
described in our common language) exists for us in fact:
it does not exist necessarily. But for other worlds we have
no language: we have no view of them: no view of our
world from them.

The Pragmatic view of religion is utterly despised by
many believers as shallow, literal-minded, self-interested.
The outright transcendentalist will say that God is outside
the world (although also within it); God is other than the
world: our understanding of God is only a glimmering:

[1] Wordsworth is a great philosophical poet because for him imagination is practical as well as reflective.

the language in which we speak of God is not literal but analogical: and as *creatures* we simply cannot begin to follow God's reasoning: what we have to do is to obey his commands. The right is what God commands. To obey is very much a matter of willing—of subjecting our will to God's will. In any other context this would be shameful: to have any true idea about religion is to see that it is the context in which this is not shameful but our only proper course: or perhaps *is* shameful but is also our proper course. By obedience we cannot become good in the sense in which God is good: we cannot avoid the evil which is in man as man. And the only escape (in life or in death) is something entirely done by God and not by man.

No doubt something like this view is to be found in much Christian theology: especially in the thought of Augustine but also in the more rationalistic views of Aquinas. It may even be true to say that a popular version of this view *is* Christianity, historically: although of course there are many hints from all periods of a more earthy and more partial view. Transcendentalism lends itself to very moving declamation: and has a wide appeal to something in us all. It has also been used by some of the most sensitive and subtle of all Christians—by Augustine and by Kierkegaard. More recently it appears that Wittgenstein thought that this was the only possible view for a truly religious mind to hold; and that although it cannot be expressed in our language, it cannot be denied either. It is indeed beyond arguments: no reasons could be given in our language which would render it in the least plausible—or implausible—'It did not please God to save his people by argument'; no argument is available for it or against it. And yet people believe in such a God.[1]

It seems odd to identify Wittgenstein with the Demea of Hume's *Dialogues*: but *some* of the views attributed to Demea are echoed in the notes which Schlick made of Wittgenstein's remarks on Ethics; and in the notes of lectures on religion given later. It is not in the least odd that Hume (Philo) should completely disagree with Wittgenstein on all these questions. If Wittgenstein ever read the *Dialogues* and the *Natural History* he would no doubt have regarded Hume's views as not merely mistaken but positively revolting: as in fact he did dislike the early views on the subject which Bertrand Russell communicated to him.

This view which is beyond argument naturally cuts a poor figure when Philo traps Demea into offering arguments. The defeat of Demea can be dismissed as the triumph of Hume's charlatan wit. But it is very difficult (it seems to me) to present the view without exposing some points from which argument seems very sure to spring. At all events it cannot be mistaken to ask just what the view itself implies.

Certainly some of the negative points are very striking and ought to be very carefully considered. (1) The metaphysical beliefs (in God's existence, in divine judgement) cannot be supported by reason. If a man does not believe in divine judgement, what would persuade him? If he

---

[1] Wittgenstein: *Lectures and Conversations* (published in 1966 on the basis of notes taken in 1938–46 by hearers): and 'Wittgenstein's Lecture on Ethics' published in the *Philosophical Review* January 1965 and belonging to 1929–30.

does believe he will perhaps make preparations for meeting that judgement. How could one begin to persuade an unbeliever that he ought to do this? (Noah could not persuade anyone to build a boat except his own family and they simply obeyed him because they had to.) The persuasive words cannot carry any weight: unbelievers have all got so many things they must do first: the judgement in no way connects with their affairs, their life, their sense of the meaning of life. The transcendental account of this is (I suppose) that what is lacking is faith: without faith the notion of a judgement means nothing— or if it is given a meaning this will have nothing to do with religion. Is any other account possible?

Hume noticed that many particular religious beliefs which people profess are not *acted upon*: people act upon other beliefs that are incompatible with their religion and simply make no attempt to reconcile them or to explain the discrepancy. He holds that the lack of connexion results in lack of real belief:

—though the vulgar have no formal principles of infidelity, yet they are really infidels in their hearts and have nothing like what we can call a belief of the eternal duration of their souls.[1]

In Hume's view, if we look wholly outside human life for an account of justice and injustice, virtue and vice, happiness and misery, the result is vacuous. The theological language has a grammar: but it has no bearing on our lives. There is no argument, no reason which can weigh with a man against the genuine practical considera-

[1] *Treatise of Human Nature*, Book I, Part iii, §9.

tions of this life. And Hume explains that these are by no means confined to a man's own life-time:

Men are everywhere concerned about what may happen after their death, provided it regard this world.

These observations are used by Hume to discredit all transcendental religious beliefs: they are used by others to show that such religious beliefs must rest upon faith and not on observation and argument. If someone tries to produce *evidence* that there will be a judgement he is not putting forward the religious view but a view to which one could properly reply: 'Well, possibly it may happen and possibly not.' And this is not religious belief. Even if some religious belief were to be supported by 'as much evidence as for Napoleon' this is not to the point: 'the indubitability wouldn't be enough to make me change my whole life'.[1]

The Fideist may very well hold that the evidence for religious beliefs (if we are to consider what is *mistakenly offered as evidence*) is altogether insufficient. It would be unreasonable to be convinced by it. This is however altogether irrelevant: the evidence belongs to the ordinary language of common discourse, history, science, everyday practice: the religious belief is outside that system altogether. Wittgenstein, if asked whether he believed in a judgement day in the sense in which religious people believe in it, would not say: 'No. I don't believe there will be such a thing.' He could not say; he could not contradict the believer.

The question how a religious person comes to be able

[1] *Lectures and Conversations*, p. 57.

to believe and to state his beliefs in a different language is not here answered. How does one come into faith? But Wittgenstein, like the Pragmatist, insists on a connexion between belief and the way a man lives. A man cannot be said to believe in Judgement Day unless he *lives for it*: and the difficulty about offering evidence for there being such a day, is partly that no *evidence* would lead a man to set aside all consideration of this life. (He will weigh the evidence: and it will be outweighed by other considerations.)

This leads to the great question: How, on this view, are we to live? Once again it is supposed not to be a matter of argument. There are people with whom on some occasions one does not argue. The religious believer does not argue with God. (Certainly this is the view of the matter set forth in God's answer to Job.) God has to be obeyed: what God commands is good. But of course we all have notions of virtue and vice which arise out of our view of society and of ourselves: we have beliefs about how we ought to live, how moral questions are to be settled. These connect with experience, reasons, arguments: they have a central place in our language. It is possible then that what God commands may conflict with all these human notions. What would happen if we were to ask which view is correct? We should be asking what reasons God has for his commands: what is the good which God hopes to secure? Butler, for example, suggests that our conscientious objection to treachery in all its forms cannot be supported by sufficient reasons from experience: but that what God had in mind in giving us this scruple, was the happiness of mankind. We cannot see, in some cases, why treachery makes for human unhappiness: God does see this. So that treachery is wrong because God has forbidden it to us: and God has forbidden it *because it is evil*.

All such arguments are rejected by Augustine and Kierkegaard (and Hume's Demea). In notes of a conversation with Wittgenstein in 1930 we find that he rejects the view that God wills the good because it is good, but has something to say for the view that good is good because God wills it.

Good is what God orders. For this cuts off the path to any and every explanation 'why' it is good, while the (other) conception is precisely the superficial, the rationalistic one, which proceeds as if what is good could still be given some foundation.[1]

Here Wittgenstein might seem to be doing no more than asserting a Kantian view: what is morally good is so in itself and not on account of any connexion with the things we desire or admire or wish to pursue from any sort of sympathy or interest. But of course Kant holds (rather precariously) that notions of moral worth as well as of what is agreeable, helpful, sympathetic and so on, exist in the sound natural understanding of man. Both concepts belong to our world.

Wittgenstein, in the *Tractatus*, went further. What is good is not *in* the world at all and to identify and describe it is not possible in our language. We have notions of good

[1] *Philosophical Review*, January 1965, p. 15.

based on interest, inclination, sympathy: these are facts of life but nothing to do with the good. And in this same conversation Wittgenstein refers to such notions as *preferences*—a wholly subjective interpretation of them. Preferences can be rationally examined, but by this Wittgenstein understands a sociological study. The good cannot be identified in this way:

The first conception says clearly that the essence of the Good has nothing to do with the facts and therefore cannot be explained by any proposition. If any proposition expresses just what I mean, it is: Good is what God orders.

Kant says we cannot identify the good by reference to the objects of inclination (human happiness and suffering, the relief of suffering and so on). Wittgenstein says the good is outside the world altogether and has *no* explanation. Perhaps Kant in fact finds no explanation, but he offers one: and one which at least purports to provide us with a rational test of right and wrong: and Kant admits the possibility of identifying moral worth in the actions of others or in actions of our own. Wittgenstein places the good *outside*. He is here prepared to say that 'Good is what God orders' comes nearest to expressing his view.

In the later lectures, Wittgenstein considers what this must mean *to a religious believer*. It means that for the believer obedience is all. Where we have beliefs which conflict with what God commands, these must rest upon mere preference, and carry no weight at all. The truly religious man, Wittgenstein is saying, will obey God *whatever* he commands: and (here is the crux of the matter) will set aside any view of his own in deference to God's command. The religious man jettisons his own notions of good and evil—they are mere preferences. The good comes altogether from outside our life, outside history: it is to us wholly arbitrary. As Wittgenstein remarks, it was not claimed by Christians that this made sense: it was claimed that it must be, to unbelievers, foolishness. Kant considers the view that the good is what is commanded by a God who is not otherwise known to be good. (And how could he be, on this view?) God has knowledge and power and majesty. To commit oneself to obedience to God is to give up one's own moral autonomy. Kant is able to say this because for him the concept of good is rational and available to men. The view that Wittgenstein is considering denies all this, without, of course, asserting that God is not, in the ordinary sense, morally good. That would be the kind of statement of which Wittgenstein would say that it neither confirms nor contradicts religious belief because it belongs to the common language and religious discourse does not. But the moral goodness of God (on this view) is simply God's *will*.

However, for the believer, God's will is to serve as a guide to his life. One who believes in the Last Judgement has to find some way of preparing himself for it. God may be thought of as transcendental: but his commands have to be carried out in the world we all share. Others may regard the conduct of the believers as foolishness: they may also regard it as heartless, treacherous and tyrannical.

What the transcendentalist view invites the believer to do, is to disregard all such objections and simply to obey God.

This I believe one could not do if one acknowledged that our idea of God arises from human needs in the world we all live in. The needs that lead a man to believe are of course not simply personal or private. They are the needs, the sufferings, the injustices of us all. I believe that religious notions do in fact spring from such needs: the moral views they express are not in fact imposed from outside but grow up within us. Consider one of Wittgenstein's own examples. In his 1930 lecture he refers to 'the experience of feeling *absolutely* safe', and remarks that this 'has been described by saying that we feel safe in the hands of God'. He is speaking of an experience which is therefore a matter of fact: and adds that it is a paradox 'that an experience, a fact, should seem to have supernatural value'. He says that the expressions he has used are nonsensical: 'For all I wanted to do with them was just *to go beyond* the world.'[1] The noticeable thing about this and other examples is that they deal with very human experiences—belonging to the world of human needs and hopes: but of course they 'go beyond' in the sense that nobody can have a *rational* assurance that he is *absolutely safe* in any sense.

The transcendental view has always also to face a second difficulty. Not only is God's will to be obeyed in this world: it has to be learned in this world. There must be this point of departure. If we cannot be persuaded by any argument life offers, just how do we learn God's

---

[1] *Philosophical Review*, January 1965, pp. 8 ff.

will? Of course the answer must be by revelation: and that something is a revelation is not a purely factual statement. How do we know that this is a revelation? Whatever answer is made, it must connote 'by faith': and the view that Wittgenstein regards as the only possible religious view cannot get any further. It can use no arguments. What then settles the question of what is revelation and what is not? Everybody knows the answer: an institution, a traditional authority, the Church. Augustine, a philosopher if ever there was one, considering the beliefs of all the philosophers, the arguments of all the schools, in the end commits himself simply to the Church.[1]

What is right in all this view is that the religious believer accepts a notion of absolute good which he cannot finally establish: and believes in the power of that good to save, to forgive, to keep in life and in death. All the *morality* of this springs from our own moral notions of integrity, compassion, justice: the confidence is the kind of confidence that a man cannot wholly explain: it meets needs of which he is not fully conscious: it is a stance which he can take and which he is lost if he does not take. Such a pragmatic faith *can* be overthrown. The need for it may go: and it is noticeable that it tends to be less or more important at different stages of life. The faith may become impossible although the need for it remains. There is the

[1] *Confessions* IX, §26: Monica, before her death, says: 'One thing there was, for which I desired to linger for a little while in this life, that I might see thee a Catholic Christian before I died.'

conversion from religion to despair as well as the conversion from religion to self-sufficiency.

Where, on this view, do religious beliefs come from? Of course from traditions and institutions which exist to meet perennial needs. These do in fact offer reasons: they are evidently not rationally compelling. Underlying the arguments is the attempt to meet a practical need. And all this is often very much better understood by men of action than by philosophers: best of all by poets.

Religions make much of the lives of certain men. Sometimes this seems absurd: sometimes they seem to have picked on a man whose life is 'an inspiring example of what men *can* do', as Mill remarks, 'but assuredly not an example of what they should'. But religions also focus our minds on the really great and on what they did, suffered and taught. And it is a *matter of fact* that we live in a world that includes such men. Time and death do not affect the goodness of good men. Religion interprets their lives and their deaths in imaginative symbolic terms: but it is still a matter of fact that a man may die to secure the forgiveness of sins. And this at all events has the absolute character of a man's giving his all. What is involved in adherence to a religion also has an absolute character in the sense that it is intended to be for life.

The traditional religions are enormously complicated imaginative constructions into which historical and natural facts or beliefs are woven. One does not invent religious beliefs: what is new in religion arises out of what is old. This means that in many ways religion is very childish. It offers reassurances very much as these are offered to children. In the stereotyped situations of life, a grown man will not need such reassurances. But life brings situations that cannot be stereotyped: facing the facts of birth and of death cannot be mere routine. All the great transitions and crises of life loom large in religion: and they are dealt with (very often) at a level which appeals to our childishness. This of course is an offence to many: but surely if we consider ourselves as we are, not as perhaps we would be, we may find this intuitive, imaginative, poetic thing appropriate.

Within any one of the great historical religions, a wide variation is found both in attitudes and in practices. The institutional powers try without much success to impose the uniformity they admire: theologians attempt to rationalise and defend. Within such a complex imaginative construction, a thoughtful man will never lose sight of the fact that it is still up to him to accept or to reject. If he is called a heretic, at all events he will not now be burned alive. And an honest man will not find himself as remote from many who disbelieve it all as from those who only pretend to believe or who accept from low motives. A man who is himself a believer cannot suppose that in the eyes of God there is a fundamental difference between those who believe honestly and those who disbelieve honestly: between those who seek God's forgiveness and those who somehow learn to forgive themselves as well as to forgive others.

INDEX